ROADS
NOT TRAVELED

Bob,
Thanks for being my
pastor, my professor,
my model, my friend.

Rick

ROADS
NOT TRAVELED

RICK IMMEL

Roads Not Traveled
Copyright © 2017 by Rick Immel. All rights reserved.

No part of this publication may be reproduced, stored in a retrieval system or transmitted in any way by any means, electronic, mechanical, photocopy, recording or otherwise without the prior permission of the author except as provided by USA copyright law.

Scripture quotations marked (NIV) are taken from the *Holy Bible, New International Version*®, NIV®. Copyright © 1973, 1978, 1984 by Biblica, Inc.™ Used by permission of Zondervan. All rights reserved worldwide. www.zondervan.com

Contents

Preface 7
Guided Tour 13
Grandpa... 33
Man Overboard! 47
It Will Be Done... 69
The Return.. 79
Missing Socks.. 85
A Father's Love 107
Bibliography 115

Preface

When I was six years old, I fell off a playground slide and broke my hip. What I remember most from the fall was not the fear, for I don't remember being the least bit scared. No, what I remember most was that it seemed to take forever for me to finally hit the ground. I felt almost like I was flying. Like Superman.

But then I did hit bottom, and I did break my hip. I now know that if I fall from that slide I may break my hip.

Looking back on it now, many years later, I see the parallel with a different kind of fall: falling in love. When falling in love, I am happier than I have ever been before. The feeling has been described as "floating on air." If something was to happen and you were to break up, then you are left with a broken heart. Just as I know that if I fall off that slide my hip may break, so do I also know that if I fall in love, my heart may break.

And although it is a joyous ride, I once found myself wondering if the pain was worth the fall.

I was sharing this thought with a friend named Paul one evening. After listening quietly, he asked, "Does your hip still bother you?"

He knew that it didn't. He was making the point that time heals all wounds. Even the amputation you feel when your heart is broken, when you feel like a part of you has been taken away.

He always said the right thing. Maybe because he always seemed to pause before he spoke to be sure of his words.

Wealth is measured not by the money in your pocket but by the number of people in whose hearts you reside. And it is becoming more and more evident to me that true wealth can only be obtained if obtaining wealth is not your goal.

I was not looking for wealth when I met Paul, but I sure could have used a friend. I feel richer having known him, even for the short time we shared together. I had answered an advertisement he had placed in the newspaper for a room he was renting in Bradenton, Florida. I moved in, and he quickly became one of the best friends I have ever had.

But even the best of friends sometimes go their own ways. However, that doesn't have to be good-bye. There is always something left behind. You always walk away with something that you didn't have when the two of you first met. Memories of the crazy things you did or the tender moments you shared. And the love you found together that couldn't have happened with anyone else.

Paul was in his midthirties, and I was seventeen. He had an IQ of 151, which was in the top 1 percent in the United States, and I was an idiot. He was attending New College, which is a division of Harvard that only admitted something like ten students per year at the time. He had been in school for basically his entire life, and he never had to pay for any of it—all academic scholarships. I had been kicked out of high school and had never gone back. Talk about an odd couple.

With all his schooling, Paul probably could have been anything in the world he wanted to be. He was not one to brag, but when I mentioned this fact to him, he paused for a moment and said sort of introspectively, as though he'd never really considered it before, "Yeah, I probably could be." He was driving a cab when I knew him. Go figure.

I remember one time Paul and I were riding Hondamatic motorcycles when a school crossing guard began to lead a line of children across the street right in front of me. I know motorcycles are sometimes hard to see, but it is her job to see. All I could do was lay the bike down and go into a slide. I watched as I very quickly drew closer and closer to the line of fourth and fifth graders crossing in front of me.

Just as I arrived at the point of impact, the crowd of children parted like the parting of the Red Sea, and I slid right through the middle of the frightened group on my side.

The crossing guard had the audacity to yell at me for being reckless. It's a miracle she didn't get someone killed.

But miracles are everywhere. They are all around us. If we only open our eyes, we can see them. Just because a miracle can be explained by science does not make it any less miraculous. I can describe how a tiny seed is transformed into a mighty oak tree, but to me, it is still a miracle.

Albert Einstein said, "There are two ways to live your life: one is as though nothing is a miracle, the other is as though everything is."

At this young age, I believed with all my heart that God existed. There was not a doubt in my heart. But there was not a doubt in my *mind* that He did not exist. It seemed impossible when I thought about all the supposed contradictions I had found in studying the Bible.

I tossed this thought to another friend one day, a Hispanic lady whom I could tell had a fire for Jesus. She smiled and, without hesitation said, "It doesn't matter what you believe with your mind. Your mind is only flesh, but your heart is spiritual."

I hadn't learned yet of Christian apologetics.

I was reminded of the story Booker T. Washington once wrote of the man who had asked a friend how the friend could possibly believe in God when God can't be seen.

The believer responded by saying, "Do you see that high-tension wire up there? You can't see the electricity running through it, but I dare you to reach up there and grab it."

But I wanted to believe it with my mind too. What I couldn't know was the many twists and turns my spiritual journey would take before I came to that belief, how long it would take to find my way back home.

I thought that, at the very least, the New Testament is a great guide for morality. It reveals the way I should behave and feel. Though I may not feel or behave in a certain way, by reading the New Testament, I know that I should. Not because God tells me I should but because everything I've ever read in the New Testament I agree with in my heart. My conscience agrees with it.

I sometimes get confused or lost when traveling down life's path and don't know which direction to take. It is at these times that I look to the New Testament for guidance. And it never ceases to amaze me how often I open the Bible in search of an answer, only to find it on the very first page I look.

There is one miracle in particular that happened to me that I would like to tell you about. I call it a miracle because there is no other way to describe what happened.

You hear people saying sometimes that they started out in life with nothing but the shirt on their backs. Well, that is exactly, literally how I started my adult life.

Guided Tour

I WAS SIXTEEN years young. As I lay in my tiny bed in the childhood home I shared with my younger brother Jamie, I looked to the ceiling in the darkness and spoke to God for what I knew could be the last time. I explained I would have to leave Him for a while to figure out what I believed on my own terms. I couldn't believe in God simply because everyone else did. I promised Him that I hoped my beliefs would bring me back someday.

As I was drifting off to sleep, I felt, very distinctly, a kiss right on the lips. It was so real that it instantly woke me up, me wide-eyed and a little unnerved. I've never told anyone that before.

This is the story of a journey that found me at various times living among squalor and in castles, standing atop summits and lying crumpled in valleys, dancing in love and writhing in agony, lost and retrieved.

It wasn't long after this heartfelt discussion with God when, at the age of seventeen, I started out on my own, headed for California. The year was 1980, and I was driving a 1969 Chevy Impala. The car was in pretty bad shape. I didn't think it would survive the trip to California I had been planning for months, so as I was driving away from my parents' home in Bristol, Indiana, I decided to change my destination from California to the nearer-by Florida, though both were a world away to my young eyes.

My leaving was a desperate attempt to start over a life that was going all wrong. I had been kicked out of school and was on probation for possession of marijuana. I was continually disappointing my parents and felt like a failure. I was ready for a new start. I knew that if I stayed in the same town I would just wind up hanging around with the same crowd and getting into trouble again.

It would be a big step for a seventeen-year-old boy who had never been more than a few miles from home before.

I left Bristol, Indiana, in early summer. Problem was I only had two and a half bucks in my pocket and less than a quarter tank of gas. I had no map and no plan, other than to follow all the signs that said south and some that said east.

First stop was Greenfield, Indiana, where my mom's family and some of my dad's were living. I didn't stop in

Greenfield to visit with anyone; it just made me feel more comfortable to see an area I was familiar with.

Somewhere in Kentucky, I got off the interstate to use the restroom, and couldn't find my way back on. I wound up on a narrow road that went up the side of a mountain. I was looking for a place to turn around when it suddenly dawned on me how majestic the view was as I went around and around, higher and higher toward the heavens.

So I just kept driving until I reached the top. The only mountains I had ever seen were the piles of snow plowed up to the end of our cul-de-sac on which we used to play King of the Hill as kids.

Needless to say, the view here was much prettier. Looking down on the tops of the trees, I wondered what other gifts the world had to offer that I wouldn't find in the tiny village of Bristol, where I had grown up.

Of course, before I even arrived in Greenfield, I had to stop for gas. I sold the eight-track tapes I had brought along on my indeterminate journey to a gas station attendant in exchange for gas. I thought the next time I needed gas I would sell the stereo, but when that time came, I couldn't find a buyer. I had to come up with a different plan.

I wound up cutting a five-foot siphoning hose from someone's garden hose in the dead of night and tried to siphon gas from a car. I had never siphoned gas before, and about killed myself swallowing so much gas. It served me right.

The only other thing I could think to do was what people sometimes did to me when I worked as a gas station attendant in Elkhart, Indiana: fill the gas tank up with gas and drive off.

I am not proud of the depths to which I sank in trying to get to Florida. I'm finding it very difficult to write about.

The first time I tried this stunt, my car stalled as I attempted to drive off. I got the engine started, and looked into my rearview mirror to see the woman standing right behind me with her hands on her hips.

I knew she had plenty of time to read my license plate number, and I was glad I had thought to put a license plate that I had stolen over my real license plate.

As soon as I was a safe distance away, I would stop and pull the stolen tag off and be on my way.

I wound up doing this twice that I can remember. The second time was at a full service station in Virginia. The attendant was hollering at me as I started the engine and drove off.

The reason I did this only twice was because God stepped in. I was driving around a long curve at night in the middle of Virginia when suddenly, the right rear crashed to the ground. It felt like the rear axle had broken.

I thought I would walk back to the nearest town and get someone to tow my car and fix it while I worked a temporary job to pay for the repairs.

When I got to the small town, I was disappointed to find that no store of any kind was opened. I began to walk back to my car, not wanting to sleep in it for fear the police would wake me up and find out I was on probation from Elkhart and send me back. I decided to grab a few things out of my car and find somewhere else to sleep.

As I rounded the curve upon returning to my broken-down car, I got quite a surprise: two police officers were already going through my car. I was walking on the opposite side of the road, and thought that if I turned around the police officers may see the change of direction I had made and suspect I was the owner of the abandoned car.

I hoped that if I walked right by my car they would assume that I had nothing to do with it. So I just kept walking. Never even looked over at my car. Walked right by.

What a lonesome feeling it was to abandon my car and what few possessions I had brought with me. I had doubted the car would make it to California but was hopeful it would take me to Florida. I knew I was on my own now, stranded halfway between home and Florida without a car or a dime to my name.

I had a decision to make: do I turn around and head back home, or do I keep going? It wasn't much of a choice, considering all I had done to get this far. And I knew the trouble that awaited me at home. I figured the police would know I stole the gas when they found the license plate in my car. I would be in even more trouble than what I already was for breaking probation by leaving town.

I also had a speeding ticket waiting for me at home that I was sure my parents had found in my dresser drawer by now. Just one more way to disappoint them. I would also be returning to the lifestyle I was trying to leave behind if I returned home.

I kept walking south, leaving behind all the possessions I had in the world in that car. One of these valued possessions was a fake rubber hand that I kept on the floorboard so that it looked as though someone was under my seat. I can only imagine the police officer's reaction when he saw and then touched the realistic hand in the dark of the night. I imagine him jumping back in a startled reaction and then getting a good laugh about it as he explained it to his coworkers.

The police wound up sending both license plates and *some* of the contents back to my dad in Bristol. They didn't even realize the one license plate was stolen. My dad figured it out though. I had forgotten about it until he mentioned it to me a couple of years later, at which point I could only smile, confirming his suspicion that I had stolen it. He once told me that sometimes people ask questions when they already know the answer. I guess that was one of those times.

My dad was somewhat also of a troublemaker in his youth, perhaps more so than me. If it runs in the family, I thought to myself, I would be in for a rough few years when I have kids.

The night I walked away from my car and its entire contents somewhere in Virginia, I wound up sleeping behind an old abandoned trailer. During this trip, I would never know how long I slept or what the time was because I had no watch. It always seemed like I only slept for an hour or two.

Somewhere in Tennessee, I was having a hard time finding a well-hidden spot to sleep, so I just lay down in the tall cool grass at the top of a small hill, with cars zipping by all around me. I was exhausted.

On another night, I came across a school bus parked out by the road in the hilly terrain of North Carolina. I decided to get some sleep inside, and settled in the second seat from the back. I don't know how long I slept, I could have used several more hours, but I figured I better get going before the bus driver showed up.

As I was leaving, I noticed that the keys were still in the ignition. This was not a good thing.

I had never driven a stick shift before, let alone a big vehicle like this, but I was exhausted and hungry and not thinking clearly, so I decided to try to drive the bus only for about a mile. Every little bit that I didn't have to walk helped.

I tried several times to pull out onto the highway, but the bus kept stalling. Suddenly, a hillbilly pulled up in a pickup truck and yelled, "What do you mean, boy?" He wasn't very happy.

I raced to the rear of the bus and jumped out the back emergency exit. I ran for a while in the opposite direction from which I wanted to go to throw him off my trail and cut across to a different road to head south again, keeping a close eye on the cars that were coming so as not to be spotted by the police.

It's funny, but the only police I saw all the way to Florida were the two that were searching my car in Virginia. Once I arrived in Florida, I immediately began seeing them everywhere.

I was out of money from early on in my adventure, which meant I didn't eat. I just kept walking. I thought that once I got to Florida I could camp out in the woods somewhere until I earned enough money to rent a place to stay.

I began hitchhiking the next day. It may sound as though I had plenty of rides, but I do believe I walked more than halfway. I remember walking through the mountains of Tennessee in the dead of night with all kinds of mysterious noises coming from all directions. That night, it was so dark I could not even see the road I was walking on. In the not-too-distant woods, wolves howled at the moon. The sound of brush being rustled helped to quicken my step.

I had read once that if you close your eyes tightly and a noise rushes straight at you, it is impossible to tell from which direction the sound is coming. It was so dark that night that it seemed like my eyes were indeed closed tightly and the nearby movement in the woods was coming from every direction.

One of the first rides I got was with a couple of high school kids in a Z/28. They were on their way to a job interview but stopped off at a liquor store to buy some wood-grain 190-proof whiskey. I thought it was a strange thing to do on the way to a job interview. As we drove at speeds over a hundred miles per hour down a North Carolina dirt road, I felt like I was traveling with the Duke brothers from Hazzard County.

When we arrived for their interview, the man asked me if I too wanted to fill out an application. I thought about it for a moment then said, "No thanks."

I thought maybe this was a sign that I was supposed to stay here. But this was not Florida. I kept walking south.

I came across a small store in South Carolina that on the front door had an amusing sign, which I had never seen before and have never seen since. It read, "Please don't spit out the door. We will furnish cups."

My next ride was with a man in a Volkswagen Bug. He was eating a spam sandwich, and offered me half. I was starving but declined his offer. You have to be careful when you are a seventeen-year-old traveling alone a thousand miles from home. I always had one hand on the door ready to jump out at the first sign of trouble.

I thought that trouble found me with the next ride I was offered. At one point, this seemingly kind old man put his hand on my thigh. I was about ready to punch him and jump out when I found out he was a minister and was traveling the country preaching at different churches as a guest speaker. It put me a little at ease, though I didn't lower my guard completely.

He wound up buying me lunch at Wendy's and gave me five dollars as we parted ways.

I only remember a few of the rides I received that summer.

Somewhere in Georgia, I got a ride with a man on a Harley-Davidson motorcycle. When he dropped me off, he handed me a card and told me to pass the word. The card read, "You have just been assisted by a member of the Full House Motorcycle Club. When we do good, nobody remembers. When we do bad, nobody forgets." I still have that card, though it received some water damage from a house fire years later.

I never stopped walking when I hitchhiked, sometimes facing toward the oncoming traffic while walking backward and sometimes walking with my back to the cars. But always I had my thumb out.

The one exception was in a park—somewhere in Georgia, I believe. I say "I believe" because I was very worn out by this time and my mind was not functioning at peak performance. I felt like David's men who fell to the ground exhausted at Brook Besor when they were chasing the Amalikites who had stolen their women and children. How spent they must have been not to be able to go after their loved ones. That park in Georgia was my Brook Besor.

I had asked someone how to get to US 75 because I was told it would lead all the way to Tampa, which I had, for some unknown reason, decided was my destination. The man I asked said that 75 was just on the other side of the park. Great!

So I started walking through the park. I walked, and I walked, and I walked. When I was done walking, I walked some more. Then I walked. The sun was beating down hotter than I could ever remember, and no one would stop to give me a ride because they were all with their families.

It has been my experience that only hitchhikers pick up hitchhikers. That is to say, only people who have had to resort to hitchhiking and therefore know what it's like will pick up a hitchhiker. Many people feel that picking up a stranger is too dangerous, and it probably is in today's society. But what all hitchhikers also realize is that it is *they* who have to be careful accepting a ride from a stranger.

Anyway, I still to this day cannot believe how big this park was. It must be one of the biggest parks in the world. My feet were burning, my lips were cut and bleeding from being so dry, and I was dehydrated to the point where I had stopped sweating.

I had finally given up on getting a ride, and for the first time, I no longer put my thumb out as cars went by. I could go no farther. I decided to just lie down on the side of the road. I say "I decided," but really, it was not a decision. I was done. I didn't know if I would wake up. Maybe I had developed heat stroke or exhaustion or something.

As I stepped away from the road, legs bent, preparing to collapse, I noticed the sound of an engine slowing down behind me. I looked over and saw a man in a pickup truck looking at me.

He asked if I needed a ride.

I simply nodded, and hopped in the back.

I can only imagine how pitiful I must have looked from behind, all wilted over and within a step or two of collapsing along the side of the road. The Bible tells us angels can come disguised as people. Maybe, just maybe…

After resting in the bed of the truck for a few minutes, I noticed a large cooler sitting next to me. I knocked on the back window, pointed to the cooler, and motioned like I was drinking. He nodded, and I opened the cooler to find what seemed like paradise. It was full of various kinds of cold drinks: beer, soft drinks, ice water. What a beautiful sight—even more so than the mountains of Tennessee I had seen a few days earlier.

I opted for a Sprite for some reason, and later wished I had just drunk ice water as the sugar from the Sprite seemed to make me even thirstier.

I could not believe how much farther I would have had to walk to get to the other side of that park. We must have driven for another twenty minutes before reaching the exit. I never would have made it walking.

When we finally exited the park, I thanked the man as graciously as I could and walked to a store to get directions to US 75. I stole a candy bar, and I hung out near the drinking fountain, rehydrating my body until they kicked me out.

Just north of Atlanta, Georgia, outside of Marietta, I got a ride in a convertible MG Midget with a man named Marc Webb. He wound up stopping by his office where he sometimes stayed all night, and he offered me some coffee. When he found out how far I had come, he asked if I wanted to take a shower. I declined, even though I must have had quite an odor by this time. Like I said, you have to be careful, and smart.

Marc had to leave for a while and told me I could rest there until he came back but asked that I please don't rip him off. I told him that I wished he hadn't said that and that he didn't have to worry.

I slept on the couch for a couple of hours. When he returned, he took me to Taco Bell and gave me a handful of change he kept in his car for the toll road. I told him I couldn't take it, but he insisted.

When I later returned to Bristol, I called him up to thank him again. He had given me his business card and asked that I let him know in the future how things turned out for me. I still have this card too. He knew me as Terry Slovik. This was the name I had started going by since I was on probation from Elkhart.

I was born in Americus, Georgia, and thought about seeing my birth town since I would be so close to it. But I wanted to travel in as straight a line as I could, and Americus would have taken me away from my course.

While I had my car, I was not as concerned about the straight line, as you can tell if you look at a map and see that Virginia, where I left my car, is not en route to Tampa, Florida—or anywhere else in Florida, for that matter—from Bristol, Indiana.

South of Atlanta, I got a ride in a semi tractor-trailer. That ride was interesting because I had never been on the inside of one of these big rigs before. The driver offered to let me sleep in the back while he drove. I declined.

He talked on his CB radio for a while and managed to get me a ride at the next truck stop with another trucker, who took me all the way to north Tampa. It was against company policy for drivers to pick up hitchhikers, so he had to find a driver who owned his own truck.

I thought that once I got to Tampa I could easily find a ride to the Gulf Coast, but I didn't get a single ride all the way through that city. It was why I decided to keep going until I got to a town where the people were nicer.

Besides, the only woods I found in Tampa where I could camp had emanating from them the deep, low rumbling mating call of the American alligator. I had no interest in mating with a gator at the time or in being a late-night snack.

I finally reached the ocean. It was in Holmes Beach. I saw that there were showers on the beaches to wash off the salt water. It was very tempting for me to get cleaned up, but I didn't have any soap or money to buy some soap. I did keep the showers in mind, though, for future use.

My next thought was to run into the ocean to cool off or just as a way of celebrating my arrival. But I knew that my clothes would become heavier and I would be worse off than before.

In Indiana, you had to pay to get onto an inevitably crowded beach, but here in Florida, beaches were everywhere, and nobody really owned them, so you just went wherever you wanted to. I was surprised to find that sometimes I would be the only person at a particular beach.

I immediately began looking for a job when I arrived in Holmes Beach, but with me being in the sorry shape I was, no one would hire me. I had body odor, bad breath, greasy hair, and filthy clothes. I must have looked like the homeless people I sometimes saw around Indiana.

I still did not see any woods that looked safe to camp in either. It was beginning to look hopeless.

I used an old telephone trick that doesn't work anymore to place a long-distance call from a pay phone to my parents to let them know I was all right. I didn't want them to know exactly where I was, so I told them I was calling from Georgia. My mom started crying, like I knew she would, and begged me to come home.

My dad, on the other hand, remained quiet and surprisingly calm, considering the circumstances. I figured he was trying to keep the lines of communication open by not making me feel that placing the call was a mistake.

I tried for one more day to find work. Worn out and starving, I finally broke down and admitted defeat. I walked and cried right out loud for hours as cars zoomed by, and finally made the decision to just lie down on a park bench out by the road in front of a grocery store and go to sleep, hoping a police officer would wake me up and help me get back home. I was exhausted, and although I felt as though I had failed, it was a relief to finally just give up.

I awoke to the sound of male voices and, for a moment, was confused. It was the police, and they asked to see some identification. I had left my driver's license at home because I wanted to conceal my identity. In my disoriented state, I gave them my alias, Terry Slovik.

They took me down to the police station until they could confirm my identity, but by the time we arrived, I remembered that my plan was to tell them that I wanted to go home. I gave them my real name and my parents' telephone number.

Here is where the miracle I mentioned at the end of the last chapter comes in. When the police got my dad on the line, Dad asked the police to call my uncle Hank who, it turns out, lived five miles from the police station!

I didn't even know I had an Uncle Hank. I didn't know I had *any* relatives in Florida. As big as this country is, of the millions of towns I could have settled in, of the thousands of miles I may have traveled in my twisted, mapless journey, how did I wind up within five miles of a relative I didn't even know existed? Especially since I was originally headed in the opposite direction, to Anaheim, California, two thousand miles away when I backed out of the driveway!

If this was not divine intervention, then there is no such thing. I truly believe I was guided to the small town of Holmes Beach, where my life took a turn for the better.

I met Paul, who had the positive influence on me I needed to gain the self-confidence I had lacked. He helped me to be more cognitive, more introspective by always asking me how I felt about situations and why I felt the way I did, not so much because he wanted to know but because he wanted me to think about it.

Paul and I did not exactly talk to each other during our late-night conversations. It was more like we *thought* to each other. He gave me the self-esteem I needed to like myself. He drove me to Sarasota, where I took my GED test and was surprised to find it to be so easy.

I received my high school diploma in the mail months before my classmates ceremoniously received theirs, and before I would have received it if I had stayed in school. Immediately after receiving the diploma, I phoned my parents.

I cannot say enough about the pain I must have caused my mom and dad by leaving or the courageous way in which they handled the situation. They had no idea I was leaving. I could not tell them because I'm sure it would have resulted in a big fight and they would have talked me out of it.

When I called my dad the day after arriving at Uncle Hank's, we made a deal. We agreed that if I didn't have a job in two weeks I would call home for a bus ticket back to Bristol.

As it turned out, I had two full-time jobs within one week, one of which Uncle Hank helped me to get.

One job was at the Cortez Lanes bowling alley in the evenings. I worked behind the machines and helped with resetting pins and returning stuck bowling balls, among other duties. It was a very boring job being back there all by myself, which is why I sometimes intentionally got the bowling balls stuck and waited for the announcement, "Ball return on lane 8," at which point I would spring into action and rescue the trapped ball. Every now and then, you would see my arm or leg dangling down above the pins out of boredom.

The job that Uncle Hank helped me get was a grueling job in a greenhouse. This was one of the hardest jobs I have ever had. I was forced to quit one day at the end of a weeklong heat wave during which the temperature during the working hours never dipped below a hundred degrees.

We had a meeting that day in which our boss told us we were visiting the drinking fountain too often and from that point on we could only go during breaks. This was before the days when everyone walked around with water. Before the days when bottles of it were sold at gas stations.

There were five of us who quit that day. I felt bad since Uncle Hank had helped me get the job through a friend of his, but he understood when I explained to him how we were getting dehydrated digging up trees in that heat.

I'm glad I got to know Uncle Hank. He was a race car driver who built his own car, which he raced on dirt tracks. He owned an auto repair shop, but the employees mostly worked on his race car. These were the same guys who were on his pit crew.

I only got to see Uncle Hank race one time. I was surprised at how much more exciting a race is when you actually know one of the drivers personally. I could imagine his thoughts and picture his facial expressions, for instance, when he was leading a race and got spun out by the second-place car. He wound up third in that race.

He wasn't winning as much in those days as he had in the past. He just didn't have the money to put into racing that most other drivers had.

A few years after I left Florida, Uncle Hank won the last race he ever entered, walked out to his car to leave, and collapsed. He was gone when they found him slumped in the driver's seat, dead of a heart attack.

He was my dad's sister's husband, and was another reason I was glad to have inexplicably wound up in Florida. I never would have gotten to know him.

Little did I know it would be another twenty-nine years before I received another sign that God had His hand on my life; after my children were grown and my daughter had two daughters of her own; after my business had run its course from meager beginnings to successful entrepreneurship to disappointing dissolution, the same outcome that had awaited my two marriages.

But God puts good people in our paths. I want to tell you about a man I once knew, a man who helped shape who I became.

GRANDPA

I NEVER MET either one of my grandpas. Not that I can recall, anyway. I do remember my mom talking about the horrible things her dad used to do to his kids and his wife. My mom had never forgiven him, even though most of her brothers and sisters eventually did.

When I was eleven years old, my mom handed me a birthday card from her dad. I had heard that he was wealthy now and assumed the card contained money, as it usually did.

As I held the envelope in my hand, I recalled the hatred my mom had for him and the grief he had caused her and my grandma.

I walked slowly to the trash can, laid the card on top of the other garbage that we were going to live without, and continued on into the living room to play.

I thought I had not given it much thought. But here I am writing about it more than a quarter of a century later.

I don't think he sent me any after that. Perhaps my mom just never showed them to me. We never talked about him much, so it surprised me when, many years later at a family reunion, my mom called me over and pointed to an elderly man seated with his back to us in a chair on the lawn a short distance away, and asked if I wanted to meet my grandpa.

It's sad growing up without a grandpa. My own children's lives are so much richer having the stories and perspectives of people with such wisdom from life's degree so well deserved. I wish I had someone like that growing up. I was looking forward to being one myself someday.

But when my mom pointed out my grandpa that warm summer day at the reunion, I again rejected the opportunity to get to know him. I just shook my head and turned away. Perhaps out of support for my mom or out of disrespect for him.

Or perhaps because the only image I had of him in my mind was from what little information I had received over the years from my mom. And perhaps this was unfair to him and to me. Now I will never know.

I grew up without cousins too. And without aunts and uncles. Oh, I had them, but they were all a long three-hour drive away. I went to visit every time my mom or dad went, which was about twice a year. Some of my fondest memories as a child are playing and wrestling with my cousins.

But it wasn't the same as other families. That could be why I have been described as somewhat of a loner. I sometimes wish I could have lived a different life. There was not a lot of happiness in my life until I reached my early twenties. I did not have a terrible childhood. I just missed out on a lot.

I remember arriving at the reunion and not even recognizing most of the people who were scattered around the lawn talking and laughing. I felt out of place, like a stranger.

It was a welcome relief to walk up to where Grandma Jack (her real name), Aunt Thelma, and Aunt Betty were seated, and have them stand to hug and kiss me. One of the matriarchs of the family actually smiled and stood to greet me upon my arrival. Even if no one else recognized me, I belonged.

For some reason, my grandma would always know me even when, for the last few years of her life, she sometimes didn't even recognize her own son, who saw her much more often than I did with my once-every-three-years-or-so visit I made when I became an adult. This meant a lot to me, that I always brought a smile to her face.

I think she always knew me because I used to make the three-hour trip to visit her at the retirement home when neither of my brothers ever did. We would sit and talk for hours, the two of us, she in her rocker, always with a faraway look in her eyes, as if she were visiting another time, another place.

All I have is a collection of small memories of her, though. I remember she would always offer me a can of pop on my infrequent visits with her. Once every few years.

On one visit, when I was leaving, I told her to stand by the window and I would drive my new car by so she could see it. Little things like that are all I remember.

It's funny, the small things you remember. Maybe if I saw her all the time I would have more meaningful memories. Maybe it's because I didn't see her often that I hold these tiny memories so dear.

Now that my wife Lisa and I were divorcing, I would like to meet someone who would enjoy having several more children with me. A glutton for punishment, some people say. A glutton for joy, I reply.

Lisa's Grandpa White, her mom's dad, is the closest thing I ever had to a grandpa. But he was already old when I met him. He had already lived a lifetime of memories.

Oh, how wonderful it was, though, to hear him recall experiences from his past with a smile on his face and see him with that familiar faraway look in his eyes.

The first house Lisa and I bought after we were married was a small cottage nestled among the dogwoods in a secluded valley near Stone Lake in Middlebury, Indiana. It rested on a tiny dirt lane just two houses down from Grandma and Grandpa White's house, and no one lived in the house that separated us.

Of course, I didn't call them Grandma and Grandpa White while they were living. I called them Leroy and Myrtle. For some reason, it just doesn't seem right not calling them Grandma and Grandpa now, after all we went through together in the short time we knew each other.

Toward the end of his life, Grandpa White became very weak with cancer. I remember this once-stocky robust man getting to the point where he couldn't even turn the key in his car door.

This from a man who worked in a rock quarry as a young man. He had been in the United States Army, and even was an amateur boxer for some time. His fingers were so big around that I think he gave up trying to find a ring that would fit. He didn't need to be wearing a ring, however, for people to know he was in love with his wife. I could see that even at their age.

Grandma White was confined to a wheelchair near the end. She had used a walker for much of her adult life. But what a contagious smile she always wore. And what a captivating twinkle she always had in her eyes.

She could not easily reach the kitchen sink, so her husband often cleaned the dishes. This was not the sort of thing a husband did in the era in which he was brought up. But Leroy was an unusual man.

He was an exceptionally strong man in his youth, short and burly. It must have been depressing for him to become as weak as he had. But I never once heard him complain.

Not once. As a matter of fact, he sometimes laughed right out loud at his predicament.

Lisa and I began doing more and more for them. I told him once that if I could borrow his riding lawn mower to cut my own grass I would cut his grass too. This made it seem to him as though I weren't doing it for him but for me, which was not entirely untrue, for I remember cutting my entire lawn with a sickle on at least two occasions.

That task would always remind me of the old movie *Sergeant York*, starring Gary Cooper. The whole neighborhood reminded me of that movie. The setting, the way everyone was always walking around and helping each other out if there was work to be done. You didn't even have to ask.

If you were cutting up a tree with a chain saw, you can bet someone would hear the commotion and show up with their own chain saw to lend a hand. Sometimes, three or four people would materialize out of nowhere and without so much as a "How ya doing?" would start cutting. And all they would expect in return was a cold beer and a return of the favor at some time in the future, when they would be hard at work on a project of their own.

All that seemed to change when Grandma and Grandpa White died. They were the center of the valley. It was him that most people showed up to help. And it was in his backyard that most folks gathered to sit and talk or just to pass the time.

She went into the hospital first with cancer. Before she was released, he was admitted with the same thing. They were both in the hospital at the same time but in different areas. She was eventually released, he was not.

Grandpa was already gone when we reached his room. Even though I knew firsthand how badly his health had deteriorated, for some reason, it never occurred to me that this might be the end, that he would be gone soon. Perhaps it was the smiles he and Grandma White always wore.

As we approached the hospital room, I was looking at the floor, carrying my daughter Sarah in my arms. I heard Lisa say loudly, "Oh, no." I looked up to see several people standing in the hall outside Grandpa White's room wearing grim expressions on their faces. That's when it hit me.

Just before he died, Lisa's mom and Aunt Patty were trying to hold his hands as he lay in his final bed. They said he seemed to be reaching out for something else. His eyes were closed, and as they tried to hold his outstretched hands, he would push them away as though they were keeping him from reaching something that he saw, or as though their touch brought him back from what he was seeing.

Finally, he smiled as though he had seen an old long-lost friend, and released his last breath.

He had said that he just wanted to live long enough to see his grandson—my son Ryan—running down the hill to his backyard. That's just about how long he lived.

I haven't figured out yet from the smile on his face if he had finally gone or if he had finally arrived.

Grandma lasted only a few months without him. It seemed as though she died of a broken heart, even though you would often see her still wearing that beautiful smile. But her eyes betrayed her. If you looked into them, you could see that even with the smile, she just couldn't wait to be with him again. The twinkle was gone.

I hoped someday I would find a love that strong. Someone I could make that happy in life.

Grandpa White was heard to say in his delirious mumbling as he lay in his hospital bed that "Rick will take care of it." No one knows what it was he was referring to, but I'm glad I could be of some comfort to him, that he felt he could count on me for something.

One of the tasks I inherited after his death was to temporarily take care of the rabbits he had recently started raising. Just before he went into the hospital, he had separated the female from the others because she was pulling hair to prepare a nest, which, of course, meant she was pregnant.

Then after his death, a strange thing happened: one of the other rabbits started pulling hair too. This wouldn't have been weird at all, seeing how rabbits like to reproduce. What made it weird though was the fact that Grandpa White only had one female rabbit.

It turns out that he had separated out the wrong rabbit. What a laugh I was sure he got out of that as he was watching over things from his seat on high.

He left his riding lawn mower to me. And his rowboat that we had used to set trotlines overnight in Stone Lake. It was legal to set trotlines in Indiana only from dusk until dawn. He taught me how.

So the two of us would row out as the sun set on Stone Lake in the evening and return at the crack of dawn, just as the mist was lifting, to retrieve our bounty.

I also learned how to hand drill a well by helping him drill his well. I am very proud of all the work I did at such a young age at the cottage by the lake. Work that included having to hand drill a well when it was discovered I could not sell the house because my existing well was positioned too closely to my septic tank.

The water tested fine, but I still had to drill a new well. It took approximately three weeks of hard work, drilling by hand every night after my full-time job. I used a heavy lead-filled contraption that I repeatedly lifted up over my head and slammed down onto each six-foot section of pipe sticking out of the ground until the pipe was only a few inches above ground level, at which point I added another six-foot section of pipe.

With each raising and slamming down of the heavy well driver, I noticed that sometimes the pipe would go down an inch at a time, but sometimes, I wouldn't see it move at all. It depended on the ground that the point was going through at the time.

Every now and then, I dropped a nut tied to a string down the pipes to see if I had reached water yet. If I had, the string would be wet, and I would have to check how far up the string the water had reached. When the water level was several feet, I attached a hand pump to see if I could pump water.

When I finally was able to pump water, I got it tested. While waiting for the results of the test, I had to hand dig a trench across the yard from the new well for the new pipes to carry the water over to the pipes at the old well, and hook the new pipes up to the old electric pump. The trench had to be deep enough to prevent freezing in the winter. I then had to install an adapter kit to the pump to convert it from a deep-well pump to a shallow-well pump.

It was a lot of work that often took me into well after dark. But what a great feeling of accomplishment to see water coming out of the kitchen faucet from an underground stream that I had tapped into with a well I drilled by hand.

Funny thing, though: during that whole three-week period that I sweated away at that project with the nightly sound of the pounding echoing through the valley, not one person showed up to help. Not one. That all stopped when Grandpa White stopped.

I did a lot of work on that little cottage. I put a wall up in the large living room to turn our one-bedroom house into a two-bedroom home, and ran heat ducts from the furnace to the new room. I put new ceiling tile throughout the house, and new linoleum and carpet. I also tore the bathroom out all the way down to a dirt floor and added a bathtub, where before we only had a shower, though I'll admit I had help with that. I built a shed complete with electricity and attached a dog pen, dug and leveled a driveway, put up a split rail fence, and chopped down over a hundred tiny to huge trees in a yard that was so dense you could not even walk through it. I had help with the bigger trees from the neighbors.

But the well is what I am most proud of. I did it all by myself with the knowledge I had gained from helping Grandpa White, and I could do it again. It made me feel like a pioneer or a homesteader living in the 1800s who moved out west to build a home and to farm the land. One of the first things they had to do was drill a well. Where there's water, there's life, as they say.

I wish I would have had someone like that to teach me those kinds of things my entire life. And to tell me stories like the one Grandpa White told about the guys who were hammering away day after day on a well, wondering when they were going to finally hit water. Their frustration mounted hourly as they kept adding sections of pipe and pounding them into the ground with no water in sight. As they sweated away the hours, one of the men looked over and noticed the point of the pipes coming straight up out of the ground a few yards away.

Now, I don't know if that's a true story, but I can still hear him laughing every time he told it.

When my son, Ryan, was born, I told everyone at the meat-packing plant where I worked that we were going to name him Joseph Leroy—after Grandpa White—and call him Joey. That's the name I thought Lisa and I had agreed upon.

When I later returned to the hospital, I was surprised to find out that Lisa had named him Ryan Joseph instead. But I understood why.

I was present when both my children were born C-section. When Sarah was delivered, I overheard the doctor say that she was a "ten." I found out later that when a child is born the staff immediately does a preliminary evaluation of the baby called an Apgar. It is a grading system that takes into account things such as breathing, heart rate, the number of fingers and toes, etc.

I had forgotten about the Apgar until the day Ryan was born. I was jolted abruptly into remembering it when I overheard the nurse say that he was an "eight."

I wondered frantically what was wrong with him, but did it internally so as not to worry his mother. I followed him to the next room while Lisa was still being operated on, and was told he had an irregular heartbeat.

A pediatric cardiologist was called in to assess how severe it was. We were told that if Ryan made it the first three days, then he should be all right.

We were horrified. Life stopped for us during those three days.

The doctor said Ryan's large size would be a big benefit. We waited.

It was during this time that my dad had come to Lisa with tears in his eyes and told her about my brother who had died as an infant before I was born. He had died of a heart problem. His name was Joey. My dad insisted it was too much of an omen for us to call our son Joey, the name we planned on calling him if we named him Joseph Leroy, and Lisa agreed.

The first week went by okay. We had to take Ryan to the cardiologist every week for a while, then every month, and then once a year. The cardiologist said Ryan's condition would never go away, that it would either stay the same or get worse, and he speculated that Ryan would eventually need open-heart surgery. He said it would be better if surgery would not be necessary until Ryan was full-grown.

He would probably not have any physical restrictions until he was in high school. This meant we would have a decision to make regarding the sports he would participate in.

Should we not let him play football and similar sports during his younger years since those are the ones he would most likely not be allowed to play when he got older? What a disappointment it would be if it turned out he really loved the sport and was not allowed to continue playing it.

So in the beginning, we started getting Ryan involved in golf and those types of sports that were less strenuous. Then we realized what a loss it would be if he were never to experience playing these other sports while he still had the opportunity.

The old saying that it is better to have loved and lost than never to have loved at all came to mind. Perhaps it was better to play football while he still could than to never enjoy the sport at all.

I wished Grandpa and Grandma White could see Sarah and Ryan now. When I close my eyes, I can see the smiles they had on their faces whenever the children were around. I wish the kids could remember those smiles.

It feels good to reflect now and then on all the little things that happened in my life that touched me, changed me, or helped make me who I am today. Things like growing up without a grandpa and like being given one later in life by an old boy named Leroy White.

Grandma and Grandpa White helped me realize that age is not my enemy, it is a trophy. They made it through life and enjoyed the spoils of a lifetime of wisdom and memories. They wore their medals proudly.

We should all keep in mind it is up to us what will be remembered when we are gone.

Man Overboard!

After my second divorce in five years, I decided one evening the best next step was to go out and get drunk. So I did just that, and I didn't come back for nine years. On the following pages are thoughts from the lost mind and soul that I had become, wandering aimlessly the landscape of enemy territory, my Sodom and Gomorrah, my Gath with its goliath warriors, where the adversary likes to hang out. Looking for a fight. Perhaps looking to get my ass kicked or looking to kick my own. I found both.

Monday, October 8, 2007

Worldwide recall on defective people.
Is it a coincidence that every time throughout my life that I've suffered the most pain, a woman has caused it?

I guess most women would say the same thing about men. Why do we do that to each other?

Tuesday, October 16, 2007

> Rainy days
> Waiting for the rain to stop
> So I can dry my eyes again.
> Waiting for the fog to lift
> So I can see clearly again.
> Wondering how my heart can be beating still
> When it's been beat up so much.

Tuesday, October 27, 2007

> Bacardi and Diet.
> I believe I'll have one more. That's the way she would have wanted it, which is precisely why we shouldn't be together.
> Think I'll stay in tonight. Drink myself a few Bacardi and Diet. That was our drink. I'm such a sap, I know. I'm so confused as to what to do. My heart says one thing, but my head says another. I've always followed my heart before, and that practice has caused me much pain. But to tell you the truth, I wouldn't want to live without that passion. The life-affirming feeling of following your heart. But damn, it hurts.

5:15 a.m.

> Okay, one more (in case anyone is following this). Maybe then I will be sufficiently inebriated enough to

sleep in an empty bed. To sleep with empty arms. Was there ever a more lonesome term? Sleeping with empty arms. Some people have not found the virtue in having someone they love nestled on their chest. Yeah, one more sounds about right.

Sunday, November 18, 2007

Each ending also marks a new beginning. I'm in the infancy of the next stage of my life, not merely the end of the previous stage. But they do overlap. Grieving the death of the previous, anxiously awaiting the evolution of the next.

Time heals all wounds, but what about amputation, when someone you love, a part of you, is taken away?

Feeling a little better—not good, but better.

Someone told me yesterday that the feeling you get when losing someone, the feeling like a part of you is missing, is much like losing a leg and trying to walk around on one leg. In the beginning you stumble. A lot. And although all you can see at first is the pain, you have to be strong because in time you will be able to look at it objectively and see truths that you couldn't or didn't want to see before.

Thanks, my friend.

I don't get it.

I don't understand me. Maybe I never will. Don't understand what drives me or what stops me in my tracks. I see it. I digest it. The flavor seems familiar to me. So why then?

12701 County Road 496. I can't get it off my mind. And I should. The home she ran to.

I'll never understand why I did what I did or why she did what she did when we supposedly loved each other so much.

Tuesday, November 20, 2007

What then?

My father once told me that if you can't live with someone, you live without them, and if you can't live without them, then you live with them. Great advice.

But what if you can't live with them or without them?

What then? What then?

Saturday, November 24, 2007

Punch-drunk.

I think I'll pass out right here, with this Corona Light in one hand and my sanity in the other. And pray.

Pray that sanity will soon win out. Or just leave me the fuck alone and let me be at peace with my demons.

As long as life doesn't become insapory to me I'll be fine. If that happens, I am lost.

Yeah, here on my floor, "Miles from Coltrane." Waiting for the day I quit kicking the crap out of myself because to tell you the truth, I've just about had all I can take.

But I know me. I'll get up. Don't turn your back on me. I'm not that easy. I can take your punch. I always get up. Always.

I think.

But I'm so tired of this crap. So tired of me doing this to myself. Beating the hell out of myself. I know why I do it. But it's kind of strange trying to defend myself against myself. When my heart's not in it. When I'm subconsciously pulling for the other guy. Feeling I deserve it. Deserving of the beating.

Saturday, November 24, 2007

I think the threads on my neck are stripped.

Just trying to get my head screwed on straight so I can stop thinking crooked. I need to let the past go and focus on today and tomorrow. Problem is I didn't want her to be a part of my past. I wanted her to be a part of my today, a part of my tomorrow, my forever. My heart still does. But the part of me I have to listen to, my head knows it would only lead to more pain.

Monday, November 26, 2007

Let karma do the dirty work.
I can't believe how good I feel. Probably because I haven't drunk in a couple days; after all, alcohol is a depressant.
Feeling motivated again. I can't say I like the mood swings that come with losing someone you love, but I do like it when it swings my way. I can see a glimpse of the old me. And I like him. Sure, he makes mistakes sometimes—we all do—and sometimes it's a doozy! But I know I'm a good person, or it wouldn't bother me so much when I screw up. Learn from it, stop punishing yourself. Let karma take care of that. Pick yourself up, dust yourself off, and move on.
And in the next breath, I say with a sigh, "Man, I miss her."

Monday, November 27, 2007

Now and then, when I am alone, I think of her.
And I know sometimes when she is alone she thinks of me.
And I like to imagine.
That once in a great while it happens at the same time, and at those moments, we are connected.

Purposes
His children revealed to him what his purpose was.
And when they were grown and gone

He wandered the earth searching for a new purpose.
And when he didn't find her
He died.

From the moment we take our first step, we are one step closer to death. One foot in front of the other; seems like a simple task. Why then do I spend most of my time backpedaling?

One breath at a time. Just breathe, right? Why then am I coughing up a lung every five minutes?

I wonder as I trot off to the store to buy another pack of bullets.

With each toke, I am one breath closer to victory.

We are all dying. Some are just doing it faster than others.

We don't reason where our feelings are involved, we just feel.

Monday, December 3, 2007

Fading.

It's interesting. I'm down to eighteen photos of her on my MySpace photo page, deleting them at a rate directly proportional to the degree that I am letting her go. Started with thirty. Slowly becoming a part of my past.

Friday, December, 7, 2007

Paging Dr. Rick.
I think I'll sue myself for malpractice. This medicine I've prescribed myself is no remedy at all. In fact, it appears to be having an adverse effect. This depressant I'm pouring down my throat to ease my pain. Maybe I'll give it a little while longer. Practicing without a license is so much fun.

Pablo, lend me an ear.
If there ever was a God in heaven, if there ever was a chance for me, let it reveal itself now. For the dawn has arrived and will not linger. Touch me not with your blasted karma—not yet. Let me stagger back to my feet so I can better battle it, better serve it, better appreciate it for the justice it provides. As of now, I see no justice. Perhaps my mind is skewed. Perhaps not. Let flow my thoughts so as to reveal my soul. And know; know that I am here. I am not going anywhere, and soon, all will be well. Or seems so in my mind.

And what else matters but what I perceive? Perception, no matter how obtuse, is all an individual has. Individual—what a novel concept when, in fact, we seem to only exist in so much as we are recognized by others.

My thoughts now arrive as though they have been delivered by a one-eared painter. Fragmented as they are, they are still mine. Ah, life. How savory, how irresistibly palatable. What will come next? I can hardly wait.

Reactions.

I am the kind of person who, if I believe something inside of me is disturbing my enjoyment of life, I will work on it for quite some time. But sometimes, how I am working on a problem indicates how I am keeping it a problem.

I agree with Hugh Prather when he wrote, "There is another way to go through life besides being dragged through kicking and screaming the whole way."

The times I can instill this concept into my psyche, I am left with one less battle I need to fight.

Run, Forest, run.

So I went jogging yesterday (in between cigarettes), allowing the crisp air to cleanse my lungs. I'm starting to get my motivation back. I like jogging. It's something I've done my entire life. There's something about the solitude, just the sound of my breathing, getting in touch with myself. And it's good for keeping my stamina up for more enjoyable physical activities (just in case that ever happens again).

Someone told me I need to stop relying on the love of a woman to feel complete. She reminded me that I was complete when I was born. I wonder, though, what good am I to myself? I can strive to be the best person I can be, but where is the worth in being good if you can't be good for someone else? I don't know, my thoughts are so convoluted right now. Good time for an epiphany. Jogging is the perfect venue to precipitate such clarity. It didn't happen this time, but I enjoyed being with myself. I think I'll go for a visit again tomorrow.

Sunday, December 9, 2007

Calmly cruising atop this glamorous ocean liner, the sun setting lazily where the blue waves meet the orange sky. Standing on deck. All seems well as seagulls dance in the sky for me.

Suddenly, a panicked shout rings out, "Man overboard!"

Salt water fills my lungs. Choppy waves whisk me farther from view. She throws me a lifeline. Gradually becoming paralyzed by the icy waters, my strength is fading.

She throws me a smile. I struggle toward it, out of breath, and hold on.

When I tell her she saved my life, she shrugs it off. "No, *you* did," she insists.

When I tell her that she threw me a lifeline, she says sincerely, "You had to grab it."

I was self-destructing, drowning in self-pity. She saved me with a smile.

I once was me.

The warm breeze persuades his wings upward toward the orange setting sun as he dives into the Pacific for his evening supper. As I stretch out in the warm California sand, I think it seems as though he does it just for my viewing pleasure. And what a pleasure it is. Does anything else really matter? You can have your *American Idol*, I'll take this. I'll die with this vision on my mind, not a box in the living room. Get it right. Live before it's too late.

December 20

A place of mind.

So I trimmed my beard in the way that once influenced someone to comment that I looked like Johnny Depp. I have also consumed about a half gallon (seriously) of rum tonight, reminiscent of the character Depp played in *Pirates of the Caribbean*.

I want to leave the seclusion of this abode, but I've got this ongoing argument with the elements. They don't like me, and I don't like them. Wish I could walk down to the beach. Or sit on the patio of some local tavern, watching happiness stroll by. And smile to myself. Yeah, that's what I wish. That I could smile. And mean it.

Just try.

This is your last moment. What will you do with it? What matters most to you? I can tell you this: when I am on my deathbed, I will not be thinking about the really cool big-screen TV I had twenty years earlier. I'll be thinking about the time my son told me with a hug that he wouldn't allow me to fail. Memories are all that we have in the end. They can take my house, my land, and my car, but they can't take my memories. I would rather spend my money on doing than on having. They can take my material possessions, but they will never have my memories. They are mine for keeps.

I'll carry you, but I can't breathe for you.

Perhaps you've heard the story before. The scorpion and the frog were standing together creek side. The scorpion needed to get to the other side, so he asked the frog for a ride.

The frog said, "I can't trust you, you'll sting me."

The scorpion looked the frog in the eye and said, "You can trust me, I really need to get over there."

The frog relented and told the scorpion to hop on. Halfway across the creek, the scorpion stung the frog.

The frog looked up at the scorpion and asked, "Why did you do that? Now we will both die."

The scorpion said, "I know, but I could not help it, I am a scorpion."

Some people will self-destruct no matter what you do to help them. That's just who they are.

Monday, December 26, 2007

Damn, my dogs are tired. They've carried me from the seclusion of the hippy hideout to the coldness of the jail cell floor. They've seen the pavement pass beneath them on a trek from the mountains of Virginia to the Florida coast. Many times they loaded me up and taxied me from Venice Beach to the Santa Monica Pier, through Palisades Park to Third Street Promenade and back again. From poverty to wealth and back again to poverty, they've chaperoned me. They helped me through the rain forest of Belize and along the coast of Mexico. Down the halls and up the ramps. Through the tunnels and over the hills. From her arms to the waiting arms of another. From crying to begging to rejoicing. And through it all, they have not failed me. But damn, my dogs are tired now.

Saturday, February 23, 2008

> Lost.
> Maybe someday…
> I will find my way home.

Tuesday, June 2, 2008

> Connections.
> I believe the most precious thing in life is time. Because you can obtain more possessions and you can earn more money, but once time has elapsed, you can never get it back.
> However, as far as importance, I think the most important thing in life is connections. Relationship connections.
> I would like to spend the remainder of my life appreciating the connections with the people I come into contact with and trying to make a positive impact on their lives.
> Or I am just inebriated and will awaken in the morning to find the same selfish loser I recognize.

Tuesday, August 5, 2008

> My life's work.
> Why did the fire have to start in that room where all my most cherished possessions were kept? Things I have written throughout my entire life, photos of precious moments or periods of my life, my shot glass collection

from all the places throughout the world my travels have taken me and which held such happy memories for me.

I can't sleep again. Every time I close my eyes, I think of something else I lost. Even a single paragraph I suddenly recall only serves to affirm that I will never remember it all.

Tuesday, March 3, 2009

Agenda:
Heading to my bros in Hermosa Beach for now. Think I'll hit Main Street in Santa Monica tomorrow, my favorite place in the world to hang out. Then Venice Beach on Wednesday. Don't think I'll do Hollywood or Beverly Hills this time, though that French restaurant on Rodeo Drive sounds good. Definitely hit Third Street promenade before I go.

Thursday, March 5, 2009

Peace Corps.
I've got a *W* today, which is more than I have in Elkhart. One *W* is better than none, right? For those who don't know what I'm talking about, which is pretty much everyone, I'll explain. I noticed a long time ago that if I have two of three Ws I'm happy. There was a time not long ago I had all three, but two was fine.

These Ws are as follows (not in any particular order): a good *w*oman, good *w*eather, and money in my *w*allet. If I have a good woman and decent weather but no money, I'm good. If I have money and good weather but no woman, I'm also fine. And so on. Two of the three Ws, and I'm happy.

Here in Santa Monica, I have the weather and money until it runs out. But in Elkhart, I have none of my Ws, except the temporary money. So my question to me is where am I most likely to find happiness?

3:23 A.M.
Friday, March 6, 2009

Peace.

What a wonderful night! After dining at Kilkenney's, which has the most spectacular view of the Pacific greeting the coast, I decided to walk along the beach on the way home. As I approached the water, I noticed the only other person on the beach was a young long-haired man sitting alone in the sand, making love to the waves with his bongos. I strolled past, wanting desperately to sit and listen, but I knew this was his moment.

A little farther down the beach, I found myself surrounded by a swarm of dancing seagulls. There must have been at least a hundred of them floating just feet from my head as the waves came crashing in, soaking my feet. And just then, I remembered why I belong here. If nothing else is going right in your life, this makes everything okay. This makes life worth living.

3:09 a.m.
Sunday, March 8, 2009

    Conflicted.
    So six hours until my flight back home. I wish people back there could experience the difference in cultures. Watching the sun set on the beach with the sound of the drum circle vibrating through my soul. I should have stayed sober for such a decision as this. Because right now, I am feeling—to hell with it. Even my mom says I've talked about living in California since I was a kid. And now my kids are grown and have lives of their own, I'm basically unemployed since giving up my business last year, so what's holding me back? I haven't found a full-time job here yet, but I have enough money to last me a couple months. That should be enough time to find a job, ya think? What to do? The choice seems obvious. God, I love it here.

4:12 a.m.
Monday, March 9, 2009

    Yeah, so I, um, cancelled my flight back. I'm still here. I'll give it a couple more days to find a job. I don't want to leave here. Maybe I'll move to tent city in Sacramento. I did get a long interview at Gold's Gym on the beach (Muscle Beach), the one where Arnold got his start. And they all have my number, and I can continue to fill out applications and send out my résumé online if, er, when I go back. Definitely have to be back in Indiana by next week, or my friend's gonna be pissed to have to go to Tennessee the following weekend by herself. I have shit I need to take care of there, anyway.

I have a squatter, for one thing. You know, a guy who comes along and sets up camp on your land. I can't get her to leave. Not my problem she has nowhere else to go. She should have thought about that before she treated me, supposedly her best friend, the way she did.

Anyway, I'm two thousand miles away, and can't get her out of my house! All right, this job hunting is exhausting, and I'm ready for a beer. I think I'll walk down to see Montana Bob at Rick's Tavern. I named him that. He calls me Indiana Rick—well, Indiana and Montana for short. Plum tuckered out.

Monday, March 9, 2009

Update: so I stopped off at Lula on my walk back from the drum circle on Venice Beach for some carne asada a la tampiquena and met a couple girls. The magician there walking from table to table was freaking us the fuck out, but in a good way. After dinner and a few drinks, we decided to walk for a couple of blocks down to Finn O' Cool's, and on the way, they asked if I was into threesomes. My answer was yes and yes. But when I found the standing-room-only Finn's was so crowded that I couldn't get served, I stepped outside for a breath and decided to stroll down to Rick's Tavern to say good-bye to Montana Bob. He's cool as hell.

So a couple of Corona Lights later, I headed toward home and stopped off at the liquor store for a half pint of 90-proof peppermint schnapps for the twenty-minute walk home. So here I am, sitting on my deck, looking at the Pacific Ocean through the palm trees, thinking to myself, Man, *a threesome woulda been good tonight.*

Sunday, March 15, 2009

What the hell is that guy wearing? And that guy? And that guy?

Another thing I love about this place is that it doesn't matter what you wear. I've seen so many outrageous ensembles that defy fashion it's just silly. I can't even begin to describe the crap I've seen worn.

I say it's silly though when, in fact, the choices being made with wardrobes are in the vanguard of the sociocultural drift.

So I check myself in the mirror before my nightly stroll up and down the strip, and my first thought is, *Do I match?* My second thought is, *I hope not.*

You are free to express yourself here, to be yourself. And the more outrageous outfits I see, the more I feel free to be me. That's how you find yourself. You can wear whatever you are. And nobody cares because they're all doing it too. In fact, they appreciate it. It makes them free to wear who they are.

So ironically, by not conforming, I *am* conforming. When the norm is not to conform, not to be normal, and people don't care or, more precisely, don't appreciate it, that's where I want to be.

2:51 a.m.
Thursday, April 30, 2009
Santa Monica

So what is it that crosses your mind just before you surrender to slumber? Is it your daughter whom you wish were five again instead of twenty-two? Is it your son with whom you swear you want to go fishing? Is it the woman whose body you wish was pressed against yours? For me, it's the sand…on the beach…on the ocean. And through the tribulations that I have had to withstand, I have withstood, anxiously awaiting the next challenge, but all the while thinking, *There's a pebble on a beach on the ocean with my name on it.*

3:23 a.m.

In the end, there will soon come a time very soon when I will no longer have the resources to blog my thoughts.

I have owned my own business for many years, and it has afforded me many nice homes, cars, vacations, etc. But now it seems to have run its course. Not a bad run for someone with no college education.

But though I haven't yet given up, I have grown very weary. As young as I am, I have seen the value in living for today. It is only life. Nothing more, nothing less.

I have but one gem of advice: follow your heart, yes, but be expectant of the inevitable. Indulge, appreciate what comes your way, but know it is only temporary. Know that going in. Everything is temporary.

When I am homeless, living on a beach in Santa Monica, know that I am happy, for I have had my run, a very successful run at times.

It is my dream. So be not sorry for me. I am not giving up here, but if I am to start over, I would rather do it in a place I love.

I will miss my friends and family, but I have to do what my heart is pulling me to do. All of my life I've known I belong to the beaches of the West Coast.

I was lost, desperately looking for the right road, not realizing I was on the right road all along. All I had to do was turn around.

I felt like I had lived an entire lifetime. I had raised two wonderful children. I had operated a successful business for eighteen years, though it had now run its course. Yet my life was only half over, so what did I do now with the rest of my life?

It's obvious by looking at the furniture-less house and the vehicle I was now driving that I was no longer a material person. I didn't care about that stuff now.

---

1 John 3:16—18.

This is how we know what love is: Jesus Christ laid down His life for us. And we ought to lay down our lives for our brothers. If anyone has material possessions and sees his brother in need but has no pity on him, how can the love of God be in him? Dear children, let us not love with words or tongue but with actions and in truth.

I was trying to find a purpose. I needed to find it.

Rick Warren wrote, "You may choose your spouse, your career, and your hobbies but you can't choose your purpose. The easiest way to discover the purpose of an invention is to ask the creator of it" (Warren 2007). I needed God to reveal my purpose.

There are plenty of ways to die. What I needed to figure out was how to live. And I needed to find it soon.

It Will Be Done

There are moments which mark my life. Moments I realize nothing will ever be the same again. And time is divided into two parts; before this and after this.

My knees were sore now, but it's a pain I was glad to have. A pain that comes from challenging hills with out-of-shape legs and traversing bridges across the St. Joe River, bridges under which I once sat to ponder life's queries from the eyes of a youth as the water flowed by like life itself. Sore from jogging past memories shaped like neighborhoods in which I used to play as a child, past houses in which I've spent time playing so many years ago where my friends used to live, friends whose parents I can sometimes glance through the windows as I jog past and who were now old and bent and some were gone. Knees sore with a pain I was almost not allowed to enjoy.

I was told I could spend the next five years in prison for punching a fireman nineteen months earlier as I drunkenly attempted to reenter my house while watching it burn to the ground destroying nearly everything I owned. Not being allowed to jog for five long years was the least of my worries at the time but one I dreaded nonetheless.

The sentence for the battery charge would be handed down at the same time as the sentence for a DUI I had received a few months before the house fire. Then instead of being locked in a cell for five years, I was told I would receive a one-year work release as a sentence. However, it was immediately commuted to one-year house arrest with an electronic monitoring ankle bracelet so I couldn't go anywhere. And now I was allowed two unexpected passes per week to go jogging. Something I wouldn't have been allowed if I had received the five years in jail or the work release.

My parents had successfully lobbied for me to serve the year house arrest at their house, my childhood home, so they could help me out with getting groceries and anything else I would not be allowed to fetch myself, though I had a feeling the true reason they pushed so hard was so I would be removed from the destructive environment in which I was living. That's the sort of thing parents do. That's the sort of thing your Heavenly Father does.

I had not had a close relationship with either of my parents, earthly or heavenly, since becoming an adult. We had simply grown apart. Now my earthly parents were elderly and not in the best of health, and after I had moved back in and was awakened by my mother's calling my name because she had fallen and couldn't get back to her feet, I realized this is where I needed to be, not just for me but also for them.

My parents.

As much as I hated being unemployed and shackled to my parents' house at my age—I felt like a grounded teenager—I knew there were benefits to, and perhaps even a reason for me being there. One, home detention had forced me to reconcile my relationship with my parents. Two, it had forced me to literally geographically be there for them to help them in case they needed me. Three, it had forced me to cease my indulgence in drinking and the subsequent destructive behavior. And four, it had aided tremendously in my spiritual awakening.

I was forced by court to attend six AA meetings while on house arrest, and though I knocked those out in three weeks, I continued attending. To be honest, the only reasons I continued going were because the home detention was causing me to get cabin fever, stir-crazy. I needed to get out of the house, and AA was one of the few places I was allowed to go. Plus, I love jogging and needed to exercise, especially being unemployed, so that I didn't sit around and atrophy.

So I kept jogging to AA twice a week, and the more meetings I attended, the more I was filled with something profound to think about, to meditate over as I jogged home, usually not pertaining to abstaining from drinking but to my spirituality. I soon realized that yes, this was a time in my life of closing doors, but more importantly, it was one of opening doors.

Sometimes, a gardener has to prune his trees so that they will not die, so they will mature and bear good fruit. This seemed to be what God was doing to me, cutting away the cancerous people and destructive situations in my life that were keeping me from maturing spiritually from my self-seeking ways and bearing good fruit. Apparently, God doesn't always give you the people you think you want, for sometimes, He gives you the people you need.

Someone asked me recently how I came to Jesus, how I came to accept Jesus Christ as my Savior. The truth is I did not come to Jesus; he came to me. He used his megaphone (pain) to rouse me from spiritual lethargy.

And it worked. I finally realized that my problems were not a punishment from God; they were a wake-up call. He whapped me with several wake-up calls before I finally opened my eyes, each one being more painful than the last.

Rick Warren once wrote, "Sometimes God uses a jeweler's chisel to shape us and sometimes, when we're real stubborn He has to use a sledgehammer." He pounded me a good one this time.

I had allowed my life to deteriorate into such a state that I literally lost it (my life) and had to be resuscitated three times, as I lay bleeding in a tavern parking lot I should never have stepped foot in, protecting a girl I should never have known.

Looking into the mirror, it occurred to me how these outside injuries seemed like a metaphoric manifestation of an injured soul. The collapsed lung reflecting the air gone out of my sails, the broken nose, a lack of appreciation for what life has to offer as I could no longer stop and smell the roses, the broken ribs a reminder that I hadn't yet finished sabotaging my own success as punishment for actions over which I felt so much guilt, the face in the mirror blue and purple with lack of recognition, a stunning affirmation that I had lost sight of the real me.

As I lay in the hospital three days later, recuperating from a beating administered by five guys whom I had never even met, it struck me that this was merely the culmination of several years' worth of wake-up calls I had ignored, pressing the snooze button and continuing my slumber through life.

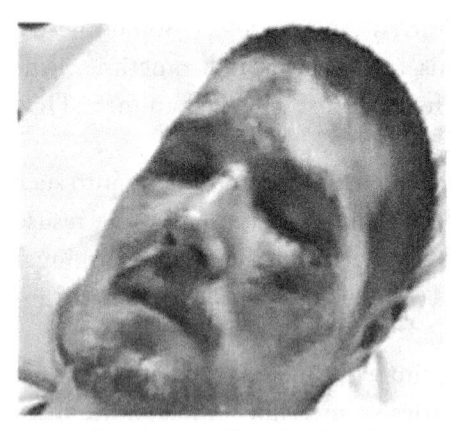

In the hospital with one of my final wake-up calls,
June 2009

So finally, one day, I stood up in church for Jesus. Pastor Mark Beeson of Granger Community Church looked me square in the eye, pointed directly at me, and said, "I agree with you."

Three days later, while sitting at a friend's apartment, God spoke to me these four words as loudly and clearly as any I had ever heard: "It will be done." I'm not sure what it meant, but I heard it. I heard it as plainly as if someone else was in the room.

So for me (though I know my senses have deceived me in the past), it's not a matter of believing; it's a matter of *knowing*, because I heard the words right out loud with my own two ears. "It will be done." These words are from the same verse in the Bible (Matt. 18:19, NIV) as the words Pastor Mark had spoken to me days earlier: "I agree with you."

Four days after hearing those words, I was baptized at Granger Community Church. Jesus had become my Sherpa, guiding me, carrying the load for me on my climb up the mountain, or, more accurately, out of the hole into which I had dug myself. The day after the baptism ceremony, I turned myself over to the police to begin serving my twelve-month house arrest.

Me with Pastor Mark at my baptism on
September 17, 2009

I've heard it said that if you always do what you've always done, you'll always get what you always got. And though what I always did had its perks, I was looking for something different now. Some people believe you can look back on your life and see forks in the road where a decision had to be made as to which direction to go, which road to take, but there are no forks. There is only one road. You're going either the right way or the wrong way. You're going either toward God or away. Pastor Mark said that too.

Nothing shapes your life more than the commitments you choose. Your commitments can develop you, or they can destroy you, but either way, they will define who you are. If you want to take the true measure of a man, see where he spends his time. I heard a man—a drunk—one time ask God why he had taken all his money. I thought to myself, *Because you're using it to destroy yourself, you fool!*

That man was me.

Change always starts first in your mind. The way you think determines the way you feel, and the way you feel influences the way you act. So in order to act differently, I must first change the way I think and thereby the way I feel. And I had done that. I had started thinking maturely, focusing on others and not myself.

It was a monumental time in my spiritual journey, a defining period. I had lost so much. I had fallen so far, but just look where I landed! I had love in my heart, love I hadn't felt in such a long time. God removed all my distractions so that he could talk to me—or more specifically, so I would listen to him. He took everything from me—my once-successful business, my beautiful house, and my tricked-out SUV, all my worldly goods, even my freedom. But he gave me a relationship with Him and restored true love in my heart. And I'll take that trade any day!

Now as I sat with my laptop warming my thighs in a bed that was a third the size of the king-size bed I gave up when I moved into my parents' home for my house arrest and not nearly as comfortable (but more so than a jail bunk), I couldn't help but think that perhaps this was God's way of mending the severed relationship I had with my parents before it was too late. Maybe it was His way of making me be there for them in their later days because if the truth be known, I probably wouldn't have been if all this hadn't happened.

I had lost my freedom to roam; the ankle bracelet ensured that (except for the infrequent passes with which I was blessed). I didn't have a job or anywhere else I needed to go, so I *had* to be there for them. I never would have been any other way if my life had not deteriorated to such a level, and I am so glad now that it did deteriorate so that I could be there for them and with them, and so that I could regain my relationship with them and with God.

For what is more important in life than relationships with your loved ones, with your children, your parents, brothers and sisters, spouses and friends, and with your God? I sit and muse as I rub my aching knees. Strange how things work out.

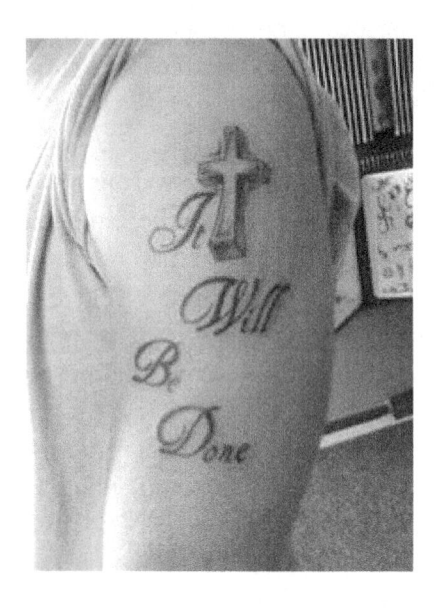

My left arm, October 2010

The Return

The bed I now lay on at the age of forty-seven as I reflected on the twists and turns of my life was situated in my childhood bedroom exactly the same as it was the night I told God when I was sixteen I would have to leave Him to decide on my own whether or not I believed in Him. I had said that I hoped to be back. Now, thirty-one years later, it suddenly dawned on me, here I am, in the same room, in the same exact location under the stars, not even an inch removed from where I was when I left God with that conversation! Back indeed, to the very same spot, restored literally and spiritually.

Who would have thought my parents would still be living in the same house and I would be sleeping in it thirty-one years later? How utterly poetic God is.

Our repentance is God's greatest joy. He will never give up on us.

This return to God in the same spot as when I left so many years before began an immediate series of signs and miracles unprecedented in my life, or anyone I knew personally, the first of which came as I jogged home in the twilight of a crisp spring evening.

Jogging is a great vehicle for prayer and meditation. Many times I would jog in the dead of winter with no cars in sight, just me and my breath clouds. Thinking, praying, listening.

It was early March, still bitterly cold in northern Indiana, and I was nearly home to my parents' house from one of my jogs to AA. Like many Americans, I had been unemployed for a couple of years since the dissolution of my office-cleaning business.

As I ran, I asked, "God, how can I do your will when I am stuck at home on house arrest, and unemployed? I understand taking away all my distractions so you could talk to me, but I've heard you, I've listened well. I understand taking away my money and freedom because I was using them to destroy myself instead of serving, but my heart is right now, and I'm ready to do your will, and I can't do it stuck at home, Lord. You have to get me out there."

Immediately following this prayer, I got the most absolute feeling that because I had asked to do His will, it would be done, just as the words I had mysteriously heard the week of my baptism six months earlier had declared "It will be done." I knew without doubt my prayer was answered.

And I smiled as I jogged. If you had driven by, you would have thought I was crazy. I'm not sure how long I smiled before I realized it, but I smiled right out loud, because I knew for a certainty something was about to happen, and I thanked God right then and there for it.

As soon as I got home, I yelled to my mom from the kitchen as she sat in the living room, "You know what, I'm going to have something to do pretty soon." She asked what it was, and I said that I had no idea but I was going to be busy pretty soon.

Mere moments later, after months and months of unemployment, the phone rang with a job offer. My faith had gotten me a job, for I was so certain of it that I already thanked Him for it. It wasn't my belief in my own faith but my belief in *His* faithfulness.

I was certain because I asked for His will; I asked sincerely for my freedom and a job so I could do *His* will. I had my heart in the right place now. I wasn't going to use my freedom and my money to walk away from God anymore but to run toward Him.

I needed money for my plans to travel to India in December to spread the glory of God there, and to Mexico in the summer to spread the Good News. I didn't want it for material things.

My probation circumstances didn't allow me to go on those trips. But I did start saving money in an envelope I kept in my room, with the words "God's money" written in big bold letters on the outside. After all, it's not our money, we own nothing. We are managers, not owners. Hearses don't pull U-Hauls, as they say, and there were no pockets in ancient burial gowns.

Progress in my spiritual growth is where I increasingly find true joy. As my relationship with my Lord grows, so grows my joy. And my peace. A peace I had no idea could exist.

It's a peace that exudes from somewhere deep inside. It's weird; I'm immersed, but from the inside out. It's a serenity, a calm that comes from surrendering to God all the various internal battles of worry, guilt, fear, doubt, and every other struggle that we as humans tend to fight and which preoccupy us and wear us down. Surrender did not weaken me; it made me stronger. If you look up the word *peace* on the Microsoft Word thesaurus, you will see one of the synonyms reads, "End of war." That's what it is to me. I'm back from the battleground, back from enemy territory. I'm home.

Peace—pure, honest internal peace—is where joy plays. It is its playground. And my King is the author of peace—the author of *my* peace.

> I am leaving you with a gift—peace (of mind and heart). And the peace I give is a gift the world cannot give. (John 14:27)

Everyone eventually surrenders to something: God, money, addictions, pride, resentment, fear, lusts. We were designed to worship God. If we fail to do that, we will find other things (idols) to give our life to.

It's hard to believe. The raging storm that was my life in recent years had its excitement, that's for sure. But the ceasefire brought with it a peace I didn't understand could exist. Now I understand.

> Every now and then you run into someone who is at great peace with himself. You can see it in his eyes; the ease with which a smile visits his face, the friendliness in which he offers it to you in greeting.
>
> He sees good in everyone he meets. He has forgiven himself all of his mistakes. He has accepted what he cannot change and does not let circumstances dictate his demeanor. He is grateful for the gift of life and has molded it into a comfortable journey. He is in complete control of his destiny, full of integrity, content.
>
> What a pleasure it is to see someone who is not fighting a great battle within. Someone who has already arrived at the destination we are all reaching out for; peace.

I wrote that when I was thirty-three years old. I am forty-seven now. Even then, years before my conversion, I understood there were people who had found something remarkable in the world, something significant. I couldn't understand it, but I knew I wanted it. Fourteen years would pass before I would finally figure out how to find it. All I had to do was turn around.

Missing Socks

There were many more signs of God's handiwork that were to come in addition to leading me to the refuge of family unknown fifteen hundred miles from home at the vulnerable age of seventeen. There was more to come than the spoken words I had heard at the age of forty-six, "It will be done," and the answered prayer while jogging on the back roads of my childhood home. God has a great sense of humor, and He loves to knock our socks off.

In December of 2010, three months after getting off house arrest, I spotted a prayer someone had written that instantly changed me. I had been worried that the loneliness from being cooped up so long would give me incentive when I gained my freedom to delve back into the murky back alleys and bars of the enemy territory of the "Gath" I had dwelled in for several years. Gath, remember, was where David fled when he was being chased by Saul. Gath is where Goliath was from—enemy territory. That's where I was during those times. That's where Satan likes to hang out. It's where he does a lot of his best work.

The reason I had originally fled to my Gath was to escape my loneliness. When I got divorced and lost the kids, I would get home from work at night and just stand there staring at the four walls. I had a close relationship with my children. My young son, Ryan, would try to wait until I got home before falling asleep. I remember he would hear me walk into his room to tuck him in when I got home, and more asleep than awake, he would reach out his hand for me with his eyes closed, and sometimes, he would whisper, "Just be, Dad. Just be." Now those moments would never happen again.

To *reave* means to take away by force. You are bereaved because you are robbed. The grave will usually plunder moments and memories not yet shared. But my treasures have been pillaged from me prematurely.

It is surely true that often our reaction to a situation inflicts more pain upon us than the situation itself. However, it is also true that our reaction to the same situation can be our greatest triumph. What I didn't learn until it was too late is that we get to choose.

I would arrive home to an empty house and couldn't stay. I had to go somewhere there were people. And the only places open that time of night were bars.

So I followed David's path and fled to Gath. I strayed far and deep and long into her bowels. And by the time the grief over losing the intimate relationship with my children had subsided, I looked around and noticed I had lost everything else too.

Home is where the heart is, and I wanted one. I wanted someone with whom I could share life, share myself, my quiet moments, my dreams, my laughter, my tears. Someone who would understand me so that I may not suffer alone, laugh alone, dream alone. Someone who would know me even as I did. Someone who would understand me even when I didn't. Someone who would accept me even when her eyes were open to all my imperfections and faults, and who would allow herself to be completely naked for me so that I may know any imperfections and faults she may have, so that I may know her dreams and fantasies, joys and sorrows. So that I may know her true self. So that I may love her for what she truly is. Someone who trusts me and our relationship this much, to be completely naked, and someone I could teach and could learn from. Someone who would always be here.

My unhealthy yearning for this person led me to some bad places in the past. And now I was feeling the loneliness again.

As I sat at my desk, I jotted down these words:

> With the passing of each day I am left one day closer to the day we will be together, or one day further removed from the days we were. One thing is for certain; it is one more day I do not get to be with her, whoever she is.

It was then I noticed this prayer a stranger had written: "Jesus is my first love, praying He will lead me to my next."

Something about those words spoke to me. And I realized that everything I already had with Jesus was more important than anything I wanted.

I dedicated this poem to my Lord and Savior: "Jesus is my first love, *trusting* in Him to lead me to my second."

I knew it was just a matter of time, that he would bring us together when we were both ready. And when I realized this fact, a great weight was lifted off me; I could literally feel it lifting off my chest and out of my head. I inhaled a deep breath as a wave of peace washed over me. I didn't have to go looking for someone to love in all the wrong places anymore.

The words I had written a few days earlier came creeping back to me, and I realized these same words could be meant for God: "With the passing of each day, I am left one day closer to the day we will be together, or one day further removed from the days we were. One thing was for certain: it is one more day I did not get to be with Him."

When I finally crowned Jesus as my first love and stopped looking for her, He stepped aside, held out His arm, and, with a smile on His face, said, "Rick, I'd like you to meet Carrie."

The very Christian woman who penned that prayer stood before me—the actual person who wrote those words I had taken to heart accepting Jesus as the love of my life!

God always answers my prayers. Sometimes, I don't understand the answer, and sometimes, the answer is no.

Sometimes the answer is "Not yet." And sometimes the answer is a simple "Okay."

It was a frosty Northern Indiana evening the following month of January. I was passing the time until I would get to see Carrie again by reading a story she had published years earlier about her favorite star, Betelgeuse. For years she would always look to the sky for the familiar Betelgeuse when the stars were out at night.

She arrived a few moments later and straightaway described how thrilled she was that her favorite star, Betelgeuse, was shining more brilliantly than she had ever seen, as though it were "dancing in the sky" as she drove to my house.

I asked Carrie how long ago she had seen it shining like that, and she said it was only a few minutes ago—the precise time I was reading the story she had written about this star so many years ago. It was dancing for her as I was reading what she had written about it.

Coincidences belong to God. It's His way of winking at us. God loves to say hi every now and then.

He smiled at us again only a month later when Carrie came to my house distressed because she had lost a lens out of her eyeglasses and had no vision insurance to pay for new glasses.

I was sympathetic but engrossed in a television program. I said, "I hope you didn't drop it in the snow, because you'll never find it," my eyes barely leaving the television.

Then out of the corner of my eye, I saw her smile a big beautiful smile, and she said excitedly, "Ya know what? God knows where it is, and when He's ready, He'll show me where it is. And I hope He does it in a miraculous way. I hope He knocks my socks off!"

Her ear-to-ear smile was understandable, because things like that have happened to her so often in the past, and her smile was contagious, because those things were starting to happen at an astonishing rate to me too: the answered prayer about the job immediately after I prayed for it, the answer to my prayer declaring Jesus my first love, and the Betelgeuse sign.

But as I turned my attention back to my television program, I said nonchalantly that usually when I lose a lens I find it in my pocket.

Carrie shook her head, and in the middle of declaring how impossible it was because she never wears that jacket, she reached her hand in and pulled out her lens. Her jaw dropped in speechless astonishment at God's signature. She had not placed her eyeglasses in that pocket—she never did—and she hardly ever wore that jacket before that day. So how did the lens get in there?

Imagine if you can: the elapsed time between her saying she hopes He knocks her socks off and to the time she found the lens was approximately ten seconds.

Like I said, God loves to knock our socks off, but it was starting to get to the point where we may as well just leave our socks off. But it gets even better.

After meeting Carrie, I was delighted to learn she was in the admirable field of home-care nursing. At the time, she had a dear old patient she referred to as Mother Abigail—after the Bible-toting character in the Stephen King film *The Stand*—because like Mother Abigail, she carried her Bible with her everywhere she went, even as she went from one room to the next in her home, almost like it was an appendage. Carrie says she could see Jesus in Mother Abigail's eyes more than anyone she's ever known.

One day, as soon as Carrie was walking in her door, Mother Abigail told her that God had told her to give Carrie a message. She told Carrie, "What God has brought together, let no man put asunder." She then told Carrie that God wants her to call her friend and tell him too. Carrie naturally assumed it was me to whom she was referring.

Carrie picked up the phone to call me, but Mother Abigail stopped her, saying, "Oh, no, dear, not now. He wants you to call him when you leave."

So Carrie put the phone away.

This message came at a time when Carrie had been praying as she drove to her patient's home over some insecurity she was feeling in her relationship with me. It occurred to her immediately upon Mother Abigail's message that this was a wonderful sign from God that Carrie shouldn't worry and that we were meant to be together. She could hardly wait to share this sign with me.

So as soon as she left Mother Abigail's, she pulled out her phone and made the call. When the phone rang on my end, I was in the middle of reading a C. S. Lewis work (C. S. Lewis, 1942). Carrie immediately recited the sentence from the Bible her patient had told her to tell me, and said confidently it was an answer to a prayer she had made moments before arriving at her house.

Carrie asked, "Isn't that weird?"

I could only respond with, "You don't know the half of it."

The sentence I had read right before answering the phone was "When a man and woman are brought together, they become one flesh." Look it up! This is the sentence in the Bible immediately preceding the one she was told "by God" to recite to me at that precise time. If she would have called sooner (when she was going to) before being stopped by Mother Abigail, or even a minute later, I would have been reading another verse or another page, or not reading at all!

Of all the things I could have been doing at that precise moment, I happened to be reading, and not only reading but also reading from the same Bible verse. The next sentence I was going to read was the one she recited. The very next sentence!

This was an undeniable sign from God that He was at work in our lives and He had put us together for a reason.

Did someone say socks? We don't need no stinkin' socks.

The two will become one flesh. So they are no longer two, but one. Therefore what God has joined together, let man not separate. (Matt. 19:5—6, NIV)

Carrie and I the week we met

It was a couple weeks later in February when I awoke with an undeniable sense of dread, like something bad was going to happen to someone I cared about, but I didn't know who.

I prayed immediately and then phoned my girlfriend to tell her about the premonition.

She said, "I hope it's not me."

I said, "Me too."

Later that night, I was driving her to the emergency room, with excruciating pain and internal bleeding. Nine hours and several tests later, we were still there. Nine hours, the two of us holding her in our arms: me and Jesus.

Suddenly, Carrie's blood pressure dropped dangerously low to 68 over 40, and she lost consciousness. The doctors immediately began preparations for surgery. At this point, I leaned over, wrapped her head in my arms, and whispered in her ear slowly, "Jesus is here, Jesus is here, Jesus is here."

After "laying my hands on her" and proclaiming my faith in the presence of Jesus, through the power and love of Christ, her blood pressure returned to normal, she regained consciousness, and the bleeding stopped on its own. An hour later, we were on our way home.

Socks? The clothes dryer can keep 'em.

Signs and miracles had been happening at an astounding pace. On March 9, 2011, as we were sitting in church, God winked at me again. I had asked God to show me a sign He was there (knowing He would). Minutes later, I received a text picture from a long-lost friend whom I hadn't seen in years. There were no words, simply a picture of Jesus doing arm wrestling with Satan.

That's God's signature. He loves to sign his work like a great sculptor or painter. And He has more socks than Fruit of the Loom. That's how he says hi to his children.

This is the picture that appeared to me minutes after I asked God for a sign He was there

Carrie and I were not without our problems, and unbeknownst to me, on this day a few weeks later, Carrie had prayed to God that if He wanted her to stay with me she would need a sign. If she didn't receive a sign by sundown, she and I were over.

That night at church, I approached the speaker Dr. Bob Laurent—he was becoming a common theme in my spiritual growth—about attending classes at Bethel College, where he is a professor. He ignored my comment and said with a smile that if Carrie and I were ever to get married we should do it in the new chapel that was to be built. Then he reached out and took my hand, placed it over Carrie's, and covered both our hands with his as he said a prayer about a mission he felt God was preparing for us. As we held hands, I felt an anointing wash over us, and she had her answer right before sundown.

There was another miraculous sign a couple weeks later. Carrie did something she never does, especially when my head is bowed in prayer at church and I'm having a moment with God. She never touches me, let alone tugs at my clothing. But now she did. And it was a quick little urgent sort of tug.

I didn't reply, however, because I was immersed in the presence of my God. Carrie and I had just commented to each other how neither of us could feel the presence of God at the service. Without telling her, I bent my head and invited Jesus. And he showed up. I felt his presence wash over me. One of those presents that make you smile a huge smile. Then I felt her tug.

She later explained why she touched me, and apologized for interrupting my moment with God. I hadn't told her yet that it really was a moment with God. She said the reason she felt compelled to touch me (and this gives me goose bumps as I write about it several months later) was because God, at that moment, was talking to her, really speaking to her about a mission He was preparing to send us on.

We were about to leave this service because we didn't feel God, but instead, I bowed my head and invited Him. It was as though He were saying, "Wait for it…wait for it… *boom*!"

At the exact moment I invited Him, He spoke to her! At the exact moment, I felt His anointing. At the *exact* moment!

God was indeed active in this church. On another Wednesday evening a few weeks later, God changed me through the voice of the speaker.

I had to help my dad install a furnace and air conditioner at 9:00 a.m. the following day but couldn't sleep all night. I was up until at least 3:30 a.m. Something about me was different, drastically. I could feel it.

Church the night before had reached me. It was unlike any of the previous hundreds of times I've been to church. It wasn't an emotional break, it wasn't a surrendering; I've been through all that. If you were there, you probably wouldn't even have noticed it. But it was monumental, life altering.

As church began and the band was finishing up and the speaker was walking up the steps to the stage, I scribbled a note to myself about living life as though I were already in heaven. I know it is up to God what eventually happens to me, but it is untrue I have no way of knowing. My salvation is up to me. I know what I have to do. It's in my hands.

Eternity has already been secured for me as a child of God through His promise. All I have to do is stay repentant following the lead of the Holy Spirit and continue to seek forgiveness for the times I don't. I am a citizen of heaven living on this earth temporarily.

Moments after scribbling this note to myself, the speaker unexpectedly mentioned these words I had just written down: "Live like you're already in heaven."

My jaw dropped. It was so astounding I was immediately transformed forever. I truly became a different entity. From this moment, this world no longer had a hold on me. I belonged to the Lord, and He knows me. Think what you will, but the exact words I had just written down were uttered by the speaker moments later. That speaker was Dr. Bob, the Bethel professor who had prayed over us months earlier.

After returning home from helping my dad, an activity that concluded with a pleasant visit with my mom, I went online and applied for financial aid for Biblical Studies classes at Bethel College, and made an appointment with an adviser.

What a day. What a first day; no longer stuck trudging along, eating leaves. I had emerged from my cocoon, and I was taking flight!

During church service a month later, I heard the speaker use the word *duplicity*. I jotted it down on a scrap of paper and stuffed it into my pocket so I could look up the meaning when I got home.

On the drive home, Carrie inexplicably, out of the blue, blurted out the word *duplicity* as we were listening to the radio. I asked why she said it. She said, "Why did I say what?" She didn't realize she had said it, and didn't even know what the word meant! I pulled the piece of scrap paper with the same word scribbled on it out of my pocket, smoothed it out, and showed it to her. Another jaw-dropping moment. There on that shred of paper was the word she had just unintentionally uttered.

Needless to say, we looked the word up as soon as we got home and didn't think it really had any significance. Later that night, we got into the worst argument of our relationship. It turns out we were both being a little *duplicitous*, and apparently, God was telling us to knock it off.

In May of 2011, one of Carrie's patients, who claimed to have the power of prophecy, told Carrie she kept seeing the word *speed* associated with me though we had never met. The next day, I read in the book *What a Way to Go* by Bob Laurent—yes, the same professor—the following:

> The things that happened in my parents' lives after Dad gave God the steering wheel could fill another book. God not only did the steering but He pushed His foot down on the accelerator as well and my folks haven't stopped racing since. Dad enrolled at Moody Bible College in spite of being six years over the age limit. (Laurent, *What a Way to Go*, 1973)

This describes me almost to a T. I had gotten the idea in my head to take some classes at Bethel College, where Bob Laurent teaches with kids less than half my age, and a mere few weeks later, I'm studying for a psych test toward my associates in Bible and Ministry. Now that's speed!

Bethel College is in Mishawaka, Indiana. As I said, the whole reason I started going to Bethel was because I was so moved by Dr. Bob Laurent when he would speak at Granger Community Church, and I knew he was a professor at Bethel. I started school by taking one online psychology class in the first summer session while waiting for the regular fall semester to begin.

With less than a week to go in the class, I had my final paper completed and was ready to submit it to the professor. However, the day I was to send it, I had read something in a book about humility, which I wanted to include in my paper. When I bought this book, *Watchman Nee: Man of Suffering* (Laurent, *Watchman Nee: Man of Suffering*, 1998), I thought it was written by Watchman Nee himself. Watchman Nee arguably did more for bringing the good news of Jesus Christ to communist China than anyone else during that time, and he suffered mightily for it.

After starting the book, I realized it was a biography written by someone other than Watchman Nee himself, but I kept reading it anyway. After reading the message about humility, I decided I wanted to cite it in my paper. I searched for the name of the author as it wasn't listed on the outside front or back of the book. I wanted to include it in a Works Cited page at the end of my paper. When I found the name of the author, I was stunned to learn the author, the person whom I wanted to cite in my psych paper, was Bob Laurent. The one person responsible for me attending Bethel in the first place was the author.

On June 18, 2011, I was struggling to save money for a mission trip to India I had felt called to go on. I hadn't started any fund-raising efforts yet because I couldn't go until the following year due to still being on probation from the whole fireman thing.

I was conflicted about the mission, however, and wondered if the money I was saving and would raise could be put to better use helping people here in my own backyard. My question was this: do I want to go on this mission for my own selfish reasons, because I think it will be cool and because it will be good for me, or do I really want to spread the good news of Jesus? I was asking God for a sign if He truly wanted me to go.

I was struggling with this question when I got a call out of the blue from my daughter Sarah who was living with her husband in Fort Campbell, Kentucky. She said she and her husband had grown disillusioned with the charity they have been tithing to, and said they wanted to sponsor my mission.

I was bursting! Here I was, asking God for a sign if I really should go on this mission or not, and my daughter calls completely unexpectedly with the money earmarked for the trip. I hadn't even started fund-raising yet and didn't even remember ever mentioning the mission to her. This was indeed confirmation from God that He was calling me to go.

A month later on August 14, 2011, I had delivered my first-ever message in a youth ministry class three days earlier. As I sat at church, the pastor began his message using the same analogy I used in mine regarding sleeping and wake-up calls. He even used the same term I used in my message, *prevenient grace*, that I had only heard used one other time in my life.

I mentioned the coincidence of these two facts to Carrie and said to her, "Now if he says something about hitting the snooze button, I'll really be impressed [by God's sign]." I had forgotten about that comment until the very end of the message, when the pastor mentioned hitting the snooze button. There was about one minute left in the message. God is poetic with this sock thing.

Only a couple weeks later, Carrie had just dropped me off at school, and we were discussing as I got out of the car that if Satan didn't want Jesus to go to the cross, why then did Satan try so hard at the trials, and why did he enter Judas?

Heading into class, I asked my professor Dr. Bob if he had time for a question, and he told me to see him after class. Approximately three minutes into the class, he asked the class the exact same question I was going to ask him and the same question Carrie and I had been discussing as I arrived at school! I had no way of knowing what he was going to talk about.

His answer to the question was, "Satan is clever, but he's not very wise." His answering my question before I could ask it was just one more sign from God I was on the right track, that I was right where I should be at Bethel.

It was September 13, 2011. I had a conversation with Carrie the night before, where upon I showed her something I had written earlier:

> Time heals all wounds. But there's no such thing as "time" in heaven. Maybe that's because there are no wounds in heaven, maybe that's the whole purpose of time; to heal wounds.

This was on my mind the next morning as I sat in class, when I heard Dr. Bob explain to the class why Jesus told the thief on the cross, "Today you will sit with me in paradise." He said it because in heaven, there is no time. The professor had said the exact same words I had said again! The proof was mounting of the Holy Spirit that the children of God all share.

In early November, the ex-roommate of me and my son was jailed for his fourth DUI. Ryan phoned me for advice because Ronnie, the ex-roommate, wanted to sell his truck to Ryan for $3,500 for bail and lawyer money. Ryan didn't need the truck but knew Ronnie needed the money.

When I hung up the phone, I prayed for God to give Ryan a sign what to do. Minutes later, Ronnie phoned Ryan from prison, and Ryan told him he wasn't sure what to do yet. While they were talking, Ryan's boss beeped in and told Ryan when he gets back to the shop there is a year-end bonus waiting for him for $5,000. Another answered prayer, the second one that day.

When we were leaving church two days earlier, Carrie mentioned, "If God is our Heavenly Father and we are His children, and He is our King, then we are essentially His princes and princesses." On this, the same day in which God answered my prayer within seconds to give Ryan a sign, one of Carrie's patients, who had never before given her a gift, was anxiously waiting for her to get off the phone with me, explaining the answered prayer that had just happened because the patient wanted to give Carrie something. It was a key chain with two words on it: "God's Princess." Two signs from God within a few minutes of each other.

My Heavenly Father was making His presence known, leaving me with no doubt I was on the right track. I couldn't wait to see what He was going to do next. He was introducing a whole new life to me, a new existence.

When I stood at chapel at Bethel College and looked out at the sea of young people worshipping the God I love so much, I was amazed. It's so easy to get discouraged with this country, the way it's turned its back on God—taking Him out of the schools, the millions of unborn babies killed every year, and so on. But now I'm shown a school where you are basically *required* to take your Bible to school. What! At most schools, you get frowned at for even saying the word *Bible*. And these kids weren't forced to come here, they chose to.

I was so encouraged to see this many young people going down a road it took me forty-some years to find. All I could think was, *Look out, Satan, this generation's coming!*

A Father's Love

The signs and the healing in the previous chapter all happened within an eleven-month period. The love and faithfulness of my Heavenly Father got me thinking about my love for my own children. The way he is shaping me day by day reminds me of how I shaped them as they grew. I could see things they couldn't see. I knew what they were ready to learn and what they weren't yet ready to be taught. But I learned as much from them as they did from me.

I remember telling them once that if they behaved and let me finish my yard work I would give them some ice cream. They were wonderful, and I was able to work well into the evening, and before I realized it, bedtime had come and gone.

I hurriedly fed them, bathed them, and got them ready for bed. Then my daughter reminded me I had said they could have ice cream. Well, I had just washed their hair, brushed their teeth, the whole nine yards, and wasn't about to give them ice cream at this hour!

So I sat them each down with a bowl of ice cream and walked into the other room for a minute. When I returned, Ryan was sitting with his arms folded, wearing an ear-to-ear grin with his ice cream bowl upside down on top of his head! He looked like a king sitting on his throne with a crown of ice cream. His six-year-old sister looked on in amusement.

I turned my head and tried not to laugh, and when I looked back, I saw my full-grown son lying on his back under his new 4×4 truck, changing his oil as my daughter shops for maternity clothes.

I blinked, and a future became memories. How did that happen? I sit and I wonder sometimes. How the hell did that happen?

When I was thirty-four, I could not imagine wanting my father to hold my hand. I didn't want him to tuck me in at night, and I didn't want to be with him twenty-four hours a day. But I could remember when I did.

And I knew that someday my children would no longer want these things from me. That's why I knew what a treasure it was when my daughter paged me just because she missed me and wanted to hear my voice. Or when my son heard me walk by as he drifted off to sleep, and without even opening his eyes, he reached his hand out for me.

What a treasure it was. How wonderful life is to offer such a treasure as this. And how cruel life is to make it only temporary, the only consolation being that it usually is not sudden, often taking years to slip away.

As the child fights for their own identity, there is a struggle within them between the part of them that wants to be independent and the part that wants to be cared for. We as parents know which side will eventually prevail.

But there are moments when he is lying in bed not fully awake, fighting for his independence, when he is half-asleep and forgetting his cause, and my son reaches out to hold my hand. And what a treasure it is, more rare with each passing day.

I wonder, is this how God feels? He knows some will not accept Him. He knows some will turn away and never come back. He knows some will choose death. Oh, how He must mourn for his children.

And how He must rejoice at the moments they are still His little children, moments when they love Him with a tenderness and honesty that can only come from a child. I was touched by one of those moments when my son was four years old. It changed me. Though it seems like a simple thing, I've never been the same.

It was Dad's Night at his preschool. We shared the night together, father and son, traveling from room to busy room. We hammered in one room, played ball in another, experimented and created in yet others.

The children had all colored ribbons for their fathers that read, "World's Greatest Dad Award." I didn't know if I could guess the one Ryan had created for me as we anxiously scanned the assortment taped to the hallway wall. We both spotted it at the same time, however. I was delighted I could recognize his before he told me which one it was. And it was official now: I am the greatest dad of all. I had a ribbon.

At the end of it all, as he was hurrying toward the door, I clutched his arm, kneeled down to look directly into his eyes, and thanked him for bringing me. I'll never forget the smile on his face and the big hug he gave me that followed. The look in his eyes of complete love was so pure, so sincere.

On the drive home, I told Ryan my favorite part was playing basketball in the gym, and asked him what his favorite part was. He said his favorite part was when we hugged. I then smiled and said quietly, "Mine too."

Sharing that tender moment with him as we drove home, with smiles stretched across our hearts, was without question the greatest thing that had ever happened to me. Ever.

I must pause here to apologize; a love this strong cannot be forced through the end of a pen.

As a young adult, I learned about life and about myself more from my children than from any other source. Parenting is a physical adventure, and that is the hard part. But it is also a spiritual adventure. Our children will grab us and squeeze us and force us to become what we are supposed to be. I didn't pretend to know at that time what it was that I was ultimately supposed to be, but I had a feeling my kids knew.

They could see what I couldn't because they weren't looking with their eyes. Sometimes you have to close your eyes so you can see, and sometimes, you have to get out of your own way. My eyesight may be weakening as I grow older, but my vision was growing stronger.

My hearing was getting better too. I remember one day we had finished supper and I had sent the kids outside to play. As I stood doing dishes, my mind drifted off to faraway times. It's funny sometimes how the smallest, seemingly most insignificant moment is sometimes remembered for a lifetime.

I suddenly noticed that the children weren't making any noise. I listened carefully for a moment then went to the door to check on them. They were fine. I had been totally engrossed in thought, yet I heard the silence. It was so loud.

God hears it too—the quiet times, times we become lethargic and aren't talking to Him. When things are going good, we sometimes grow comfortable and get lazy in our worship. God hears it. The neglect. And He has no qualms about rousing us from our indifference. God will do anything to get us to heaven, but He won't force us.

God sees it when we turn away and start walking down the road in the wrong direction.

A child can have a good home life and a loving, supportive family but he can still get confused. That doesn't make them a bad person; it makes them a confused person. It makes them human.

I went through it as a child with my earthly parents and again later as a child of God. And through it all, my earthly parents and spiritual father remained faithful.

We as parents don't require our children to be perfect. Likewise, our Heavenly Father knows we are incapable of being perfect until He has finished with us. But He expects us to try. And to ask forgiveness for the times we aren't perfect. Like Jonathon's son Mephibosheth in 2 Samuel 9, our seat at the royal table does not have to be rescinded because of our imperfection. His seat was his seat not because of something he did but because of a promise made to Jonathon by the king (David).

I remember the day I stopped weary and weathered, head tilted toward the dusty dirt road upon which I stood contemplating the long path that lay ahead. With my shoulders slumped in exhaustion, I slowly turned and lifted my eyes to see if there was a different direction.

And my Heavenly Father saw me. When His son—lost in the barren wilderness for so many years—turned around and looked at Him, He saw my face. He saw the sincerity in my eyes. And He leapt for joy as He watched me turn. And He ran to me, and before I could even begin to recite my speech of shame, He wrapped His strong arms around my head and pulled it to His chest and wept with joy at my return. Just like any father would do.

"So he got up and went to his father. But while he was still a long way off, his father saw him and was filled with compassion for him; he ran to his son, threw his arms around him and kissed him" (Luke 15:20)

Every once in a while, who you are comes face-to-face with who you should be. It's a defining moment when it happens. The decision you make at that precise moment will reveal your true identity, your honest character. There are only two things you can take to heaven when you go: your character and the people you lead to Christ.

I had come face-to-face with that person I was meant to be when God thought me up and I realized I was meant to be a child of my Heavenly Father, a father who remained faithful to me through all my wandering through enemy territory. It was time to start being the person I was when He thought me up.

Do you feel the same tug? If you do, you should follow it. And do it soon. Time has a way of talking us out of things. You are as close to Jesus as you want to be; if you are not closer, it's not his fault. That's on you.

> He is no fool who gives what he cannot keep to gain what he cannot lose. (Eliot 1958)

That's a powerful statement. It is not foolish to give up this life (which can't be kept) to gain a life that can't be lost (eternal life). Whatever we have to do in this short life to obtain eternal life is certainly worth it.

So stop wasting your salvation. God has a task for you: to love the next person He sets in front of you, and the next, and the next. You can give without loving, but you cannot love without giving. The Bible tells us we are put here to do good works (Eph. 2:10). What you do for yourself dies with you. What you do for another lives on forever in the people they in turn affect.

Jesus would not be the Messiah if not for his healing, his calming the seas, his walking on water, his fulfilling prophecies, his dying for our sins, and his rising three days later. Don't just be a human being, be a human *doing*. Too many people think Christianity is about what you don't do. They're wrong. It's more about what you *do* do. You're on the right road. Turn around.

> For we are God's workmanship, created in Christ Jesus to do good works, which God prepared in advance for us to do. (Eph. 2:10)

Bibliography

Eliot, J. *Shadow of the Almighty*. 1958.

Laurent, B. *Watchman Nee: Man of Suffering*. Barbour Books, 1998.

Laurent, B. *What a Way to Go*. David C. Cook Publishing, 1973.

Lewis, C. S. *The Screwtape Letters*. HarperCollins, 1942.

Warren, R. *The Purpose Driven Life*. Zondervan, 2007.

Made in the USA
Monee, IL
20 February 2024